ISBN 978-1-331-29540-2
PIBN 10170385

# 1 MONTH OF
# FREE
# READING

## at
## www.ForgottenBooks.com

By purchasing this book you are eligible for one month membership to ForgottenBooks.com, giving you unlimited access to our entire collection of over 700,000 titles via our web site and mobile apps.

To claim your free month visit:
www.forgottenbooks.com/free170385

# Similar Books Are Available from
# www.forgottenbooks.com

# THE WAY OF CHRIST

*TEN STUDIES IN DISCIPLESHIP*

---

ALEXANDER C. PURDY

# The Way of Christ

*Studies in Discipleship*

ALEXANDER C. PURDY

BIBLICAL DEPARTMENT, EARLHAM COLLEGE

THE WOMANS PRESS

600 LEXINGTON AVENUE

NEW YORK CITY

1918

# CONTENTS

# PLAN OF THE BOOK

This book is meant to lead the reader directly to the Bible. It is for this reason that certain references grouped under the head of biblical material stand at the beginning of each chapter. A number of questions designed to open up the biblical passages follow. These references and questions should be thoughtfully studied *before* the material of the chapter is read.

The chapter itself will then tend to gather up the results of the personal study and focus the attention upon certain definite points which may then serve as profitable topics for group discussions.

An outline for group discussion is appended at the back of the book for the benefit of the leader, and the purpose of the study is there indicated.

# CHAPTER I

## THE "SET" OF A LIFE

### SUGGESTIONS·FOR PERSONAL STUDY

**Biblical Material.**

1. Read Luke 1:5, 6; 46-55, 67-79. Try to characterize this group of people.

2. Look for evidence of Jesus' acquaintance with the great prophets; Cf. Isaiah 29:13 with Mark 7:6; Hosea 6:6 with Mt. 9:13; Isaiah 61:1ff with Luke 4:16ff, etc.

3. Read and study Luke 2:40-52.

### I. The Importance of Getting a Good Start.

1. Read the preface of Luke's gospel (1:1-4), noting the care with which he has selected his materials. Why did he pick out this one incident (Luke 2:40-52) from the early years of Jesus' life?

2. When is Jesus usually said to have begun his life work? Is there any sense in which we may say that He began his life work before his entrance upon the public ministry? In what sense did He begin his life work as a boy of twelve?

3. Why was it important that Jesus set the compass of his life so early?

4. Why is a good start of such importance in any field of endeavor? Why is it important from the point of view of the individual? Of those with whom he lives? Of the task he may have to do?

9

## II. What Constitutes a Good Start?

1. Name the elements which entered into Jesus' experience in the temple. Which was the most important, his home training, his own awakening understanding, or a sense of the world's need?

2. Just what did Jesus *do* to start his life work? What is the significance of the silence of the records at this point? Was this "start" marked by outer achievement or inner attitude?

3. What constitutes a good start for any life? Is there any world need to-day comparable to the need of Jesus' world? Is there any "hope" to-day as widespread as the Kingdom hope in Jesus' day?

## I. The First Picture of Jesus.

We know almost nothing about the boy Jesus. Just a few sentences sum up the story of the first thirty years. Into those obscure years of his boyhood and young manhood legend and myth have sought to peer, but the gospel history grants us only one clear picture. Luke, the artist of the evangelists, has drawn it for us with a few swift strokes of his pen, and it is a priceless treasure. We could not do without it, for the features of its central figure are drawn with such sure, firm lines that we know Him better from this single picture than a score of less revealing sketches could have told us.

Read again the familiar story of the boy Jesus in the

temple (Luke 2:41-50). We have reason to be thankful for it, not because it shows what an abnormal lad Jesus was to be there listening to the deep talk of theologians and asking them from time to time questions that amazed them. Jesus always had that gift. He could ask questions that searched honest men's souls and bared the plots of scoundrels and it is not so astonishing that as a boy of twelve He had that faculty. Most twelve-year-olds ask questions that go straight to the heart of things and leave older folk with no adequate answers.

But read on. He becomes so interested in what these graybeards are talking about that He actually forgets the home journey and the home-going kinsfolk, and the hour set for departure comes and goes. His parents leave, thinking Him in the company. They discover their mistake and hurry back to find Him in the temple sitting at the feet of the rabbis, listening to them and asking questions. Then, the half hesitant reproach, "Son, why have you treated us in this way? Think how anxiously your father and I have been searching for you!" And He turns to them, this twelve-year-old peasant boy, and asks, "Why have you been searching for me? Did you not know that I must be about my Father's business?" It seems a strange answer. Can we hope to understand it and the boy who uttered it?

## II. What People Thought About Religion in Jesus' Day.

Was Jesus' reply to his parents simply the answer of a strange and wonderful boy, with a halo around his head? May we not come at it from another angle? What could those graybeards have been discussing as they talked there in the temple—the latest scribal interpretation of what

Rabbi So-and-so had said concerning Rabbi So-and-so's explanation of a dry-as-dust legal tradition? Such talk would never have caused any boy to forget father and mother and home. But there was one subject which would enthrall every earnest Jewish boy,—the Kingdom, the coming Kingdom.

Just as so many hearts are athrill with the hope of a coming world democracy to-day, so the coming Kingdom was the dream of every Jewish patriot and the hope of every pious home. It was the silver thread woven into the dark fabric of Jewish history. In the blackest night great prophets told of the dawning of a better day when David's glorious reign should be equaled and indeed surpassed, and Messiah should come to rule the world and restore the Jews to their rightful dominion. What other subject could have engaged the thoughts of those wise theologians and that eager peasant boy? What more natural than that the boy Jesus should have asked, When and how will this day come?

There were Pharisees among the teachers in the temple that day, and we know pretty well how a spokesman from that party would have answered the question. "The kingdom," he would have replied, "belongs to another world order than this. We cannot bring it in by political revolt against Rome or by social revolution, for it is the Kingdom of the age that is to be. We know not when it will come, but this we do know, that it will be inaugurated by signs and portents. The sun will be darkened, the moon will become bloody, the stars will drop from their places. There will be a terrible catastrophe. The forces of Jehovah will battle victoriously with the evil spirits and then will the new world come. It will be let down out of the heavens upon the earth. Messiah will rule upon the throne of David and the sons of Abraham will inherit the kingdom prepared for them. All our enemies will have been slain by the sword of Jehovah, and the Jewish nation, revived, restored and glorified, will come into its own. And if we hope to share in this glorious day we must be good Jews. Observe the law with scrupulous exactness, every jot and tittle. And the traditions of the elders and the interpretations of the scribes, these are of vital importance. Tithe and fast and pray and sabbatize with meticulous care."

And then perhaps a representative of the sect of the Essenes, clad in spotless white, would speak. "I agree with the Pharisee as to the nature of the Kingdom and its coming," he would say, "but that we may prepare for participation in it we would do well to withdraw from the world with its sordid cares and material ambitions and live in meditation and prayer. Ceremonial purity is essential for entrance into the coming Kingdom and one must renounce worldly concerns and business affairs, trade, gain and the like."

There might even be a Sadducee present who would venture to speak. His remarks would run like this, "I care little for theology. It's a mistake to fill the heads of the people with such wild ideas as these. I take no stock in any fanciful notions of a coming Kingdom. Affairs are going well as they are. So long as the Sadducees hold the priesthood, the nation is in good hands. The poor will always grumble, but it is the part of wisdom to make the best of things as they are. Rome is a powerful state and we had best live on good terms with her. The Sadducees are setting the best example."

Only voices such as these would have been heard in that group that day, but they were not the only voices in the

Palestine of Jesus' day. Though but a boy, He would have heard in Galilean Nazareth and on the journey to Jerusalem the cry of the poor. "Oh, that some deliverer would appear! We common folk would hear him gladly. We would make him king and follow him in any attempt to cast off the Roman yoke and set up a Jewish political state here and now. The Pharisee and the Sadducee can afford to wait and speculate about a Kingdom in the far distant future, but we, who feel the burden of poverty and who know what it is to be hungry and cold, want relief now."

And still another voice would be sounding in Jesus' ears as He listened to the scholars in the temple that day. He would be remembering the hopes and ideals of the home circle from which He had come. The quiet, devout spirit of Mary, his mother, and her kinswoman, Elizabeth, would not be forgotten. He would have been told of the words of Zacharias (Luke 1:68-79) and of the aged Simeon (Luke 2:29-32). We need to remember when we think of the Jews of Jesus' day that they were not all like the formal Pharisee and the worldly Sadducee. The first pages of Luke give us a picture of very different folk, simple and devout. They named their sons after the old Hebrew patriarchs. Note the names of the sons in Jesus' home: James (or Jacob), Joseph, Simon, Judas (Mt. 13:55). In such quiet lives the noblest spirit of the Old Testament lived on.

The boy Jesus would be thinking, too, of the lessons He had learned in the village synagogue school. The great opening words of the Jewish confession of faith, "Hear, O Israel, Jehovah our God is one Jehovah, and thou shalt love Jehovah thy God with all thy heart, and with all thy soul, and with all thy might" (Deut. 6:4), were perhaps the first words He had been taught to repeat. He would be remembering the words of the great prophets with their insistence upon justice, mercy, love and righteousness, such words as Amos spoke, "Hate the evil and love the good and establish justice in the gate" (5:15); and Hosea, "I desire goodness and not sacrifice, and the knowledge of God more than burnt offerings" (6:6); and Micah, ". . . what doth Jehovah require of thee but to do justly, and to love kindness, and to walk humbly with thy God" (6:8); and the new covenant of Jeremiah (31:31-34); and the Servant Poems of Isaiah.

Is it too much to suppose that ideals and hopes were the subject of discussion in the temple that day and that widely divergent opinions were even then confronting the boy Jesus? See how such a background lights up the puzzling answer He gave his mother.

### III. The Dawn of a Great Purpose.

And He said to them, "Why have you been searching for me? Did you not know that I must be about my Father's business?" The halo fades from the picture. We no longer see the boy Jesus in the dim half-light of magic and mystery. His is neither the wan, drawn face of an ascetic nor the precocious face of a prodigy. But Luke has drawn for us the earnest, strong features of a manly peasant lad. It is a face alight with hope and glorified with a dawning purpose. He is saying to his father and mother, These things I have been hearing, and the noble prophetic ideals and the hopes which you have told me of at home—all this is my Father's business. And to-day I know, as you, too, cannot help knowing, that I must be about this, my Father's business. This is to be my life task.

15

It is not given us to know how much or little He under-stood of his own life that stretched out before Him, but these were the words He spoke. The compass of his life was set. He could return now to Nazareth to be "obedient to them."

## IV. The Silent Years.

For eighteen years He lived in Nazareth. Not a word do we have from the records about those years save the very general statement of Luke that He "advanced in wisdom and stature and in favor with God and man." Yet we may picture the Jesus of the silent years with reasonable certainty, for his teaching and life during the three years of public ministry reveal what manner of boy and man He must have been in Nazareth of Galilee.

They were years of labor. We have been wrong in think ing that his trade was an aside which merely occupied his hands while brain and heart were up in the clouds. In all probability He was a builder of houses and not simply a small carpenter who did repair work in his father's shop.

"His interest in the foundations of the temple, his parable of the houses built on the rock or on the sand (Mt. 7:24-27), his allusions to the destruction of the temple and to its being rebuilt (John 2:19, 20), to the man who pulled down his granaries that he might build larger (Luke 12:18), and to the builder who exhausted his resources before completing his work (Luke 14:28-30), all imply that Jesus was a master builder " *

We may picture his social life in that small city, Nazareth.

* Kent: Life and Teachings of Jesus, p. 55.

Nowhere is there a better chance of coming into contact with all kinds of folk, genuine and hypocritical, generous and selfish, queer and conventional, than in a small town. Was it in these years that Jesus acquired his marvelous knowledge of human nature? Men do not suddenly learn after reaching the age of thirty years to be equally at home with rich and poor, learned and ignorant, nor are they welcomed at wedding feasts if for thirty years they have been living hermit lives. Jesus must have known and liked his townspeople and in turn He must have been liked by them.

We may with all confidence think of Him as rejoicing in the great out-of-doors in these eighteen years, for as Paul loves illustrations from cities and soldiers and athletics, so Jesus' teachings are full of birds and flowers and fields.

We may think of Him as in close touch with the larger world of men. Had He world problems to face in those silent years? Was He confronted with anything comparable to the surging world issues which challenge young people to-day?

"It has been a common mistake to think of Nazareth as a quiet spot far from the life of the great world, where Jesus was nurtured in seclusion. That is far from the truth. . ... The smiling waters of Galilee lay scarce more than fifteen miles to the east. Only a few miles farther to the northwest was the Mediterranean. Nearby ran, north and south, the great highway which for centuries joined the ancient kingdoms of Egypt and Babylonia. . . . Just below, to the south, was the great plain of Esdraelon, where so many of Israel's battles had been fought. All about was the teeming life of Galilee with its numberless villages and cities. . . . From the hills above his home He must have seen at times the

Roman legions on their march, and Roman rulers with their brilliant following." *

Nazareth was far less provincial in its interests and associations than many an American city.

But what of his inner life? Did He sometimes ask Himself during those long years, When will my time come? As He stood at dusk or sunrise on the hills above Nazareth and looked out over the Galilean plains or caught a glint of the blue waters of the Mediterranean far to the northwest, did He ask, Will all my life be like this? Did He sometimes forget the great purpose which He had expressed in those boyhood days of awakening understanding? No, He never forgot or wavered. How do we know? Because when his hour struck He was absolutely ready. When the call came for a larger service, He heard a voice saying, "Thou art my beloved Son, in Thee I am well pleased." Well pleased at what? we may ask. He had neither preached nor healed nor ministered in any public way. He must have been well pleasing to his heavenly Father in the unrecorded toil as a carpenter, in his daily dealings with the people of Nazareth, in the commonplace routine of daily living. Even there He felt the imperative to "be about my Father's business."

This single purpose dominated his life from first to last. Always the direction of his life was the same. As the little trickle of water gathers moisture from this slope and that and widens, deepens, broadens, growing in power and momentum until in majesty it pours its mighty waters into the ocean, so through Jesus' life there flowed this stream of purpose, broadening, deepening, widening as the years went on

* Rall: New Testament History, p. 36.

but ever making in the same direction, his Father's business, his Father's will for Him.

## V. The "Set" of a Life.

The first picture we have of Jesus reveals Him as a boy who at the age of twelve had a single clear-cut purpose. There is not the slightest hint that He knew where that purpose would lead him, nor is there a suggestion that He had a solution to offer for the tangled religious and political problems of the day. He was but a lad, and the marvelously revealing story which Luke has left us does not picture Him as rebuking the Sadducee or correcting the Pharisee or sympathizing with the Revolutionist. But He did hear the call of the Kingdom, and in response to that call He promised but one thing for the needs of humanity and that was— *Himself.* He gave the supreme gift that any human being can offer to the world,—an unexhausted, untainted, potential personality, strong with the strength of gathering energies, buoyant with the hope and promise of youth. That was his gift when He said, "I must be about my Father's business."

Our study is to be about citizenship in the great democracy of God that is to be, but so far we have not explained who the citizens are or indeed what constitutes citizenship. Ought we not to begin by defining and discussing and speculating about these things? Or, on the other hand, was this just the mistake the Pharisees made? They put theory and theology first and personal dedication to the needs of the world and the cause of righteousness, second. Jesus reversed the order. He gave his life to the cause of God and let that lead Him where it would. He was not committed to any theory or program save the program of God as that would

19

unfold itself to Him through the eighteen years of obscurity which followed.

Citizenship to-day begins where Jesus began, with a personal dedication to the things that are right and clean and true, to the things the world needs, to the things of God. It involves in the first instance not the acceptance of a theory but simply the resolute "set" of the soul toward the "right as God gives us to know the right." A goodly heritage and high ideals, a rich background of home influences, these values are as priceless to-day as they were when the boy Jesus first faced the great world and its need, but they are not enough. Behind all this, using it all and building upon it, there must be an unswerving personal purpose. If there be such a regnant purpose in the beginning of life, men and issues fall into line behind it or are judged by it and rejected.

The man or woman, though neither brilliant nor talented, whose life is organized by a sufficient purpose, moves steadily through the years, making every opportunity for study, every bit of experience, every social and athletic achievement, every single individual encountered, pay tribute to that purpose. There is not a human vocation which does not call for such singleness of aim. The initial achievement for any task is not the mastering of the task but the mastering of the self, the "set of the soul" to some sufficient goal.

It is not otherwise in the Kingdom of God.

> "One ship drives east, another drives west
>   While the self-same breezes blow.
> 'Tis the set of the sails and not the gales
>   That bids them where to go.

"Like the winds of the sea are the ways of the fates
  As we voyage along through life,
'Tis the set of the soul that decides the goal
  And not the storm or the strife."

## VI. The Purpose Tested.

If we are to form any true estimate of the power and
meaning of Jesus' boyhood purpose, we must look for just a
moment down the vista of the years, those three tumultuous
years. Through what a maze of passion and human need,
hostility and adulation, triumph and disaster, He moves un-
disturbed! Temptations real and powerful assail Him. He
checks them up with his purpose. Has this anything to do
with God's plan for me? He seems to say. If not, He sweeps
it aside. It is powerless to touch Him. Easy popularity lies
within his grasp but He deliberately rejects it, because personal popularity in itself does not mean the accomplishment
of his purpose. Just as deliberately He antagonizes the most
powerful forces in the land because they block the way to the
accomplishment of that purpose.

He moves among social outcasts and moral degenerates
but they do not pollute Him; rather He saves them. With
equal freedom He associates with people of wealth and cul-
ture and they do not rob Him of his purpose or cause Him
to "ease down."

Even the last terrible temptation to turn aside from the
path which leads to the Cross prevails not. "He steadfastly
set his face to go to Jerusalem" (Luke 9:51).

"He steadfastly set his face"—these words constitute an
epitome of his life. He was mastered by a mighty purpose,

21

a consuming, dominating, organizing purpose. As a boy of twelve, little comprehending, perhaps, what was before Him, He uttered the words, "Do you not know that I must be about my Father's business?" In the garden of Gethsemane, after He knew it all, He said, "My Father—thy will be done."

To seek to understand what those three tumultuous years in the life of Jesus have meant to humanity and should mean to us to-day—this is the purpose of our study.

# CHAPTER II

## THE BEGINNINGS

### SUGGESTIONS FOR PERSONAL STUDY

Biblical Material.

1. John the Baptist.
    a. His birth and silent years. Luke 1:5-25, 57-80.
    b. His ministry. Mt. 3:1-12, Mk. 1:1-8, Luke 3:1-20.
    c. His last message, Mt. 11:2-11, and his death, Mt. 14:1-12.

2. The baptism of Jesus. Mt. 3:13-17, Mk. 1:9-11, Luke 3:21-22.

3. The temptation of Jesus. Mt. 4:1-11, Mk. 1:12-13, Luke 4:1-13.

### I. Preparing for Citizenship.

1. Characterize John.

2. In what way did his silent years differ from the silent years of Jesus? How did his wilderness experience fit him for announcing the Kingdom?

3. Suggest some reasons why John was simply the great herald of the New Order and not a citizen of. it (cf. Mt. 11:11).

4. Recalling the contrast between the silent years of Jesus and John, enumerate the different elements which make up an ideal preparation for citizenship in the New Order.

## II. The Call of the New Order.

1. Look for the principal points in John's message. Just what was it that drew Jesus to John?

2. Does John's message meet the world situation to-day, with regard to the hope of a new world order, the desire for social and political justice, the need for Christ-like leadership?

3. Grapple with the problem of what Jesus' call meant to Him. Is there a sense in which conditions to-day constitute a like call?

4. How are the temptations of Jesus typical of our temptations as we face worthy life aims? Is the temptation to self-gratification real in daily experience? How does popularity constitute a temptation? Think of concrete ways in which the temptation to compromise manifests itself.

## I. The Herald of the New Order.

> John, than which man a sadder or a greater
>   Not till this day has been of woman born:
> John, like some lonely peak by the Creator
>   Fired with the red glow of the rushing morn.
> —F. W. H. Myers.

The name John carries with it a certain atmosphere of rugged sincerity and strength, of honesty and serviceableness. No single individual ever did more to give this common name its honest fearless sound than did John, "the Baptizer," who from his desert solitude stepped into the midst of men with a challenging message which caught the attention of all Palestine.

He was known in those days for his own sake, but we must always think of him in connection with Jesus. And perhaps it is by setting John over against Jesus that we shall come to understand him. Like Jesus, John had breathed in the quiet, devout spirit, the earnest expectations which characterized the very finest type of Jewish home (Luke 1:5-25; 57-80). He must have known how his own birth had been associated with the noblest patriotic hopes of the day (Luke 1:15ff and 68ff).

But aside from this, the lives of Jesus and John were sharply contrasted. John's father was a priest and as a boy he doubtless spent long hours studying the priestly lore, while Jesus during those same years was learning the builder's trade. John lived in the "hill country" of Judea (Luke 1:39), where nature was far more severe than the friendly Galilean country. Judean hills made men independent and fearless, but they did not tend to draw them close together. At any rate, John left the haunts of men and went out into the desert "till the time came for him to appear publicly to Israel." (Luke 1:80, Weymouth.) And during those days and years when Jesus was leading the busy life of a master carpenter in Galilee, John was alone in the desert, feeding his soul on the sterner elements of Old Testament prophecy. His school was the solitude, his companions the wild beasts, his teacher the God of the prophets of old.

When John broke silence he quickly became the outstanding figure of the day. Like the great prophets who had gone before him he was extremely sensational. He could afford to be sensational because he had something to say. Prophecy was a mission, not an occupation, with John. Just as Isaiah caught the ear of the Judean grape growers by appearing as a ballad singer with the song of his friend's vineyard (Isaiah 5), just as Amos must have drawn rounds of applause by condemning Israel's unpopular neighbors (Amos 1, 2), so John got a hearing by appearing in the uncouth garb of the wilderness (Mk. 1:6), strangely like the dress of the great Elijah (II Kings 1:8), whose return, many believed, was to usher in the Kingdom.

Instantly there was tremendous excitement in the land. Crowds flocked to hear him (Mark 1:5). And the message he had to give was no less sensational than his appearance. It was no pleasant word, for as he saw these multitudes pouring out from Jerusalem and all Judea he did not say, "I'm glad to see so many of you here to-day." Rather, he pointed out their sins. "O vipers' brood, who has warned you to flee from the coming wrath?" (Luke 3:8, Weymouth) were the words he used to describe the Pharisees. People must have winced under the lash of his tongue, but they stayed to hear and be baptized, common folk, proud Pharisees, aristocratic Sadducees, for there was a compelling authority about this prophet and he had something to say that thrilled every heart.

## II. The Message of John.

The remarkable outpouring of people to hear this rude man of the desert was due in the first place to his announcement that the Kingdom of God was at hand. It was a *call to hope*. That was a welcome word to every Jew. It meant that Jehovah was coming to judge the nations and to deliver his people; that the hated Roman rule was to be cast off and

Israel restored. There were many who longed for "the day," there were some who may have timidly believed it was close at hand, but here was a ringing authoritative voice announcing its imminence.

Yet John's message was more than a call to hope, it was a *call to conscience*. With stinging words he cut into their national complacency and racial exclusiveness. They were given no opportunity to gloat over the reversal of things which was to be—Jew exalted, Roman subjected—for like a pistol-shot rang out John's word, repent! "Repent," said John, "in view of the coming Kingdom! Get ready! For judgment will not be upon Gentiles alone, but upon Israel." This call to conscience was disconcerting, but underneath the layers of formalism which the Pharisees had superimposed, the moral genius of the Hebrews still lived. They heard again the great formula of the prophets, Religion means Righteousness. How it challenged them Luke graphically tells us.

(In the Weymouth translation) :—Accordingly John used to say to the crowds who came out to be baptized by him, "O vipers' brood, who has warned you to flee from the coming wrath? Live lives which shall prove your change of heart; and do not begin to say to yourselves, 'We have Abraham as our forefather,' for I tell you that God can raise up descendants for Abraham from these stones. And even now the ax is lying at the root of the trees, so that every tree which fails to yield good fruit will quickly be hewn down and thrown into the fire." The crowds repeatedly asked him, "What then are we to do?"

"Let the man who has two coats," he answered, "give one to

the man who has none; and let the man who has food share it with others."

There came also a party of tax-gatherers to be baptized, and they asked him, "Rabbi, what are we to do?'"

"Do not exact more than the legal amount," he replied.

The soldiers also once and again inquired of him, "And we, what are we to do?"

His answer was, "Neither intimidate any one nor lay false charges; and be content with your pay" (Luke 3:7-14, Weymouth).

The herald's task was not complete. It was inevitable that his message of hope and righteousness should arouse the latent Messianic expectations of the people. There were questionings on all sides. "Is this Messiah?" (Luke 3:15.) Finally the queries reached the ears of John. Picture his dismay! In shocked surprise he shrinks from the idea. "Not I, not I, but mightier than I is the coming one." All the stern elements of prophecy which the lad John had learned at his priestly father's feet and had found congenial in his desert solitude burst into flame as he sought to picture the coming Messiah. Read Luke 3:16, 17. As we try to fit this picture to the life of Jesus, we read a deeper meaning into the words of John's Gospel, "And I knew him not" (John 1:31). Truly John did not understand the One who was to come, but in his own self-abnegation he sent forth the last great note of his herald's message, *a call for leadership*.

## III. An Estimate of John.

The John of the Judean hills was not adequate for the constructive task of building a new World Order. He saw the flaws in the Old Order,—the narrow complacency, the superficial religiosity, the want of common justice and mercy, and he condemned it fearlessly and with tremendous effectiveness. And when his task was done, with a humility as rare as it was fine, he voiced the need of all humanity for a Leader, and stepped aside. Like Amos, who came from the same Judean hills, he gave his message and retired into the shadows. He had finished his task.

` The greatness of John cannot be a matter of doubt to him for whom the words of Jesus are authoritative. In the midst of Jesus' ministry, John sends from his prison cell to know if Jesus is really the Coming One (Mt. 11:2, 3). The mission and message of Jesus seem of such a different nature than he had expected. Jesus sends back an answer well calculated to relieve his perplexity, and then, turning to the crowd, He seems to defend John against any charge of weakness or indecision, in striking words of eulogy:

(In the Weymouth translation):—When the messengers had taken their leave, Jesus proceeded to say to the multitude concerning John,

"What did you go out into the desert to gaze at? A reed waving in the wind? But what did you go out to see? A man luxuriously dressed? Those who wear luxurious clothes are to be found in king's palaces. But why did you go out? To see a prophet? Yes, I tell you, and far more than a prophet. This is he of whom it is written,

"'SEE, I AM SENDING MY MESSENGER BEFORE THY FACE, AND HE WILL MAKE THY ROAD READY BEFORE THEE' (Mal. 3:1).

"I solemnly tell you that among all of woman born no greater has ever been raised up than John the Baptist; yet one who is of lower rank in the Kingdom of the Heavens is greater than he (Mt. 11:7-11, Weymouth)."

John's tragic end came as the result of his fearless denunciation of the sins of Herod (Mt. 14:3-12), and the words which follow in Matthew's gospel (14:13) add a beautiful and touching note in their portrayal of Jesus' sincere grief at the death of his friend. It was at the tidings of his death that Jesus turned from the multitude and with the little group of the inner circle sought solitude. Could they have done otherwise than quietly talk together of this herald of the New Order, and his life of service?

## IV. John and Jesus.

We last saw Jesus in Galilean Nazareth, engaged in the absorbing tasks of a builder, moving acceptably among his neighbors, responding to the busy life of that small city, yet not unaware of the greater world of men and its complex problems. We thought of his inner life during those silent years and wondered if that glorious boyhood purpose was ever crushed by the weight of common tasks and by the dullness of routine. Did He ever ask, When will my time come?

And now we have the answer. At the age of thirty, in the full consciousness of mature powers, having realized the promise of those early days in physical, intellectual, social and spiritual development, Jesus of Nazareth

"——placed the tools in order, and shut to
And barred for the last time the humble door."

His time had come.

No single event in his life is more fascinating than this call to a larger service. The call came to Him in a simple and natural way and yet irresistibly. John's was precisely the type of message to which the boy Jesus of the temple, now grown to manhood, must needs respond. John's *call to hope*, "The Kingdom is close at hand," was the very note which had set Jesus' face steadfastly toward his Father's business back there in the temple. The hope of a New Order would challenge Jesus from every viewpoint.

Think how the vision of world democracy, the thirst for a lasting and righteous peace, the hunger for social justice, is moving all men of good will to-day! Was it something as deep and powerful which moved Jesus when John's urgent call for the coming of the New Order sounded out? But even more would he respond to John's *call to conscience*. A moral reform was stirring in little Palestine, and even in Galilee its influence was distinctly felt. Galileans were flocking to the Jordan, undoubtedly Jesus' own neighbors among them. Pharisees had talked about a New Order to come. What could one do about it? Nothing, except to keep the law and the traditions. But John had a different answer to that query. What can one do? Get ready for the New Order. And that means clean hands and pure hearts. It was in confession of their sins and in genuine desire to be morally fit that so many Jews submitted to "the Baptizer's" simple rite. Think you that Jesus could stay in Nazareth when a movement like this was on foot?

But more compelling than the urgent, authoritative note of hope and the clear challenge to the conscience, was that other thrilling note in John's message, the *call for leadership*. "Are you Messiah?" they asked of John. "Not I, not I,"

31

he answered, "but One mightier than I is coming, whose very sandal strap I am not worthy to unfasten." May not Jesus have felt already stirring within Himself the consciousness that his Father's business led in the direction of the fulfil ment of John's lofty anticipations? Was He to be the great leader of this New Order?

## V. The Father's Business.

Thus it came about that Jesus stood one day with the others on the banks of the Jordan. Mark tells what happened in language so severely simple and concise that it becomes the most impressive of the gospel accounts. It is as though the writer were saying, "This is what took place. The event itself is so tremendous that it needs no adornment or expansion in the telling."

(In the Weymouth translation) :—At that time Jesus came from Nazareth in Galilee and was baptized by John in the Jordan; and immediately on 'his coming up out of the water He saw an opening in the sky, and the Spirit like a dove coming down to Him; and a voice came from the sky, saying,
"Thou art My Son dearly loved: in Thee is My delight" (Ps. 2:7; Isa. 42:1). (Mark 1:9, 10, 11, Weymouth.)

Think how this incident found its way into the gospel record. Perhaps Jesus Himself first revealed its inner meaning. Who else could have known? Months afterward, when He had turned from the public ministry in Galilee and was giving all his time and thought to that little group of follow ers, He unfolded to them in beautiful symbolism the significance of that day.

## THE BEGINNINGS

What did it mean for Jesus? Shorn of the imagery so difficult for the western mind, it stands forth clearly as the beginning of Jesus' life work. That day Sonship came to its vocation. As the boy Jesus had known with unmistakable clearness that his life was to be spent at his Father's business, so Jesus in the full maturity of his perfect manhood, knew what the Father's business was to be and his own place therein. The Father's business which should claim his life was the bringing in of that New Order which John had heralded. From the moment of the baptism Jesus' life and teaching center about the coming of the Kingdom of God, the new World Order which was the dominant hope of all men of good will.

How close home it brings Him to our own day! God's business on this earth has always been the establishment of a new and better order of life, and Jesus, nineteen centuries ago, gave Himself to that task. This humble peasant mingled with the throng and went down into the muddy waters of the Jordan in unreserved dedication to this tremendous hope.

It was revealed to Jesus on that day not only what his Father's business was to be but his own place therein. His was to be the place of supreme leadership. John's call for a leader had not been in vain. Jesus of Nazareth was the answer

The words in which the heavenly message has come down to us are significant. "Thou art my son dearly loved: in thee is my delight" (Mark 1:11, Weymouth). They come from two Old Testament passages, both expressive of the age-long hope of the Hebrews, and yet so strangely different that our thought is challenged by the contrast. The first phrase, "Thou art my son," is a quotation from the second Psalm. The picture is that of Israel's ideal king.

> Jehovah said unto me, Thou art my son;
> This day have I begotten thee.
> Ask of me, and I will give thee the nations for thine inheritance,
> And the uttermost parts of the earth for thy possession.
> Thou shalt break them with a rod of iron;
> Thou shalt dash them in pieces like a potter's vessel.
> (Psalm 2:7-9.)

Compare John's striking picture of the "mighty" one (Luke 3:9, 16, 17). Power, majesty, dominion, almost ruthless in its severity—these are the characteristics of both pictures. Was Jesus such a leader? Now turn to the other phrase, "in thee is my delight." Apparently this phrase comes from the forty-second chapter of Isaiah.

> Behold, my servant, whom I uphold; my chosen, in whom my soul delighteth: I have put my spirit upon him; he will bring forth justice to the nations. He will not cry, nor lift up his voice, nor cause it to be heard in the street. A bruised reed will he not break, and a dimly burning wick will he not quench: he will bring forth justice in truth. He will not fail nor be discouraged, till he have set justice in the earth; and the isles shall wait for his law. (Isaiah 42:1-4.)

Does this fit more accurately the life of Jesus? What a paradox is here: mastery, dominion, power, on the one hand; service, patience, suffering, on the other. May we not seek to understand as we see his life and teaching unfolding, how

Jesus solved this paradox and revealed the way to mastery through service, and to Lordship through suffering?

'At least three things are clear about Jesus' baptismal experience. First, He dedicated Himself unreservedly to the New Order and its coming as the business of his life. Second, in that act of dedication He received a call to the supreme place of leadership in the New Order. Third, something of the nature of that leadership was made clear to Him. It was to gain its potency through service to the point of suffering, that justice and truth might be the possessions of all nations.

## VI. The Temptation of Jesus.

The temptation is but the reverse side of the supreme experience we have just been studying. Read the vivid accounts in Luke and Matthew (4:1-13; 4:1-11). Once again we have Jesus' own account to his disciples, for no one else could have told it. The picture language conveys like a flash to the brain of the Oriental meanings that we gain only through more prosaic channels, and here Jesus is evidently using graphic symbols to describe his temptation experience.

Mark tells us that it was the "Spirit" that impelled Him to go out into the desert (Mark 1:12). Fired with an intense desire for the coming of the New Order, He sought the solitude that He might commune with that Father whose business now engaged his whole thought.

How should the New Order be inaugurated? How might He win men to it and still preserve its fair and just ideals? The temptations came in connection with real life problems. They are the temptations that assail all manhood and

womanhood as it faces worthy life tasks, and they constitute one of the strongest bonds that bind Jesus to his fellows.

In reality the temptation is but one, though it shows three
beads. It is a temptation to lack of faith in God and his
way. Jesus, through the very passion of his longing for
the New Order, felt the force of every short cut or apparent
substitute for God's own way of bringing it in. But in
each instance He resolutely put the tempting program aside,
committing Himself anew to the will of God.

In the first phase of the temptation He reaffirmed his
allegiance to the fundamental law that self-gratification has
no place in the New Order. It may cause full stomachs
for the few but it means empty souls for the many (Mt.
4:4). See with what insistence Jesus proclaimed that law
of the New Order throughout his teaching (Mt. 16:24; Luke
12:16ff). Is that a necessary law in the New Order that men
dream of to-day?

The next phase (Mt. 4:5ff) was the temptation to gain
a following by spectacular means, by catering to the ideas
of the time. How passionately Jesus yearned that men in
large numbers might enlist in the New Order! (Mt. 23:37.)
Why not gain a quick popularity? But He saw the difference between an outward following and a spiritual allegiance,
and chose the harder, longer path. The New Order must not
be based upon insecure foundations.

And finally (Mt. 4:8ff) He set his face against all compromise with evil, knowing that not only does the means
fail to justify the end, but that He who adopts wrong means
never reaches the right end. Once again He declared his
unswerving devotion to the cause of God in the world.

"So the devil, having fully tried every kind of temptation

on Him, left Him for a time" (Luke 4:12, Weymouth). Luke in his phrase "for a time" suggests that these temptations recurred. Jesus had won the first victory for the New Order, and from this time forth He marked out its course in perfect alignment with the Father's will.

## VII. The Beginnings of the New Order.

For nineteen centuries these events, the preaching of John, the call and temptation of Jesus, have meant to Christian people no less than the beginnings of a new and better order of life upon this earth. John with his challenge to hope, to conscience and to leadership, Jesus with his dedication to that hope, his acceptance of that leadership, and his victorious allegiance to the divine purpose and plan—these have marked out the lines along which all progress toward the better order has moved.

To-day in sorrow and pain, hatred and bitterness, service and sacrifice, the hope of the New Order is rising like an incoming tide in the hearts of men.

fellows.
rs three
and his
ing for
apparent
But in
n aside,

ned his
ion has
tomachs

hat law
t; Luke
lat men

to gain
e ideas
men in
23:37.)

egiance,
iust not

ll com-
means
· means
red his
rld.

# CHAPTER III

## THE STATESMANSHIP OF JESUS

### SUGGESTIONS FOR PERSONAL STUDY

**I. Jesus' Wisdom in Beginning the New Order.**

1. Review Chapter II and see how Jesus began his work by linking it up with a great popular movement. Do you think Jesus could approve of everything in this popular movement? What things could He approve of?

2. Compare John's picture of the coming Messiah and Jesus' own idea of his mission, as set forth in the preceding chapter. How did these ideas differ? Now read Mk. 1:14, 15. What agreements between John and Jesus do you find here? Are there any differences?.

3. Read John 4:1-3. What do these verses indicate concerning Jesus' relations with John?

4. From the foregoing questions, summarize Jesus' attitude toward others and their ideas. Was it constructive or destructive? Was He looking for points of agreement or points of difference?

5. Test your own attitude toward others. Do you make more of points of agreement or points of difference? How far is it possible to ignore differences?

**II. How to Deal with Apparent Failure.**

1. Read John 2:13-22; 2:23, 24; 4:1, 2. Note the elements of failure in these references—hostility from religious

leaders, superficial acceptance by many, danger of friction with John. Read Mt. 23:37 as a summarizing statement of Jesus' experiences in Jerusalem.

2. These disheartening experiences came to Jesus at the very beginning of his ministry. How did He adjust his work to them? He could "give up" or "go on blindly" or "look for an open door." Which did He do? Read the simple statement in John 4:3. Was He giving up all hope of Jerusalem or simply waiting for a better opportunity and seeking a more receptive field?

3. What hints for the individual who faces apparent failure are to be found here? Which is the part of wisdom, "to give up" or "go on blindly" or "to look for an open door"?

## III. How to Deal with Opposition and with Popularity.

When Jesus left Judea and began his Galilean ministry He faced both popularity and opposition. Read Mk. 1:28, 37, 38, 45 for evidences of the great popularity He aroused in Galilee. Glance over Mk. 2-3:6 for evidences of decided opposition.

1. Read Mk. 3:13-19 Jesus accepted the popularity as long as He could help the crowds but He did not value it too highly, and chose a smaller group to whom He could impart his real message.

2. Read Mk. 4:10-12. See how He sifted the crowd by means of parables in order to attract only those who were genuinely interested. Moreover, the parables did nothing to increase the hostility of the religious leaders.

3. How much is popularity worth? Is it an end in itself or a by-product? How is genuine popularity acquired? Is

it possible to gain popularity by direct effort? What are the tests of popularity? Is antagonism unavoidable? What would the experience of Jesus indicate? How far should one go in avoiding hostility?

### IV. The Statesmanship of Sacrifice.

Read Mk. 8:31-38, esp. vs. 35; John 12: 23, 24.

What is the final test of devotion to a cause? What is the convincing power of willingness to die for a cause? What are the values worth dying for? How many are included in the New Order of Christ? How is it possible to express one's willingness to die for Christ's Kingdom where the demand is to live a commonplace, undramatic life? What does it mean to lose one's life in a cause?

The New Order outlined by Jesus needs not only citizens but statesmen, and as Jesus Himself is the ideal citizen of the New Order, so also He embodies those qualities of statesmanship which must characterize Christian leadership to-day.

We rarely think or speak of Jesus as a statesman. We meditate upon his perfection of character more than upon his practical handling of the actual problems of life. And yet the latter is a part of the former. We think of his goodness more than of his wisdom. Yet his keen insight into the conditions of his own day and the marvelous way in which He gave his message so that men could never forget it, are worthy of the same careful study which we give to his deeply spiritual messages.

Jesus was a statesman of the highest type. Without

formal education in either statecraft or religion He launched a· movement destined to affect all subsequent history. He was bitterly opposed by both church and state. The powerful religious leaders of his own people, supreme in all religious matters and all but supreme in civil affairs, tried their best to crush this Galilean. They set in motion all the political and ecclesiastical machinery at their command. They exerted every energy to make Palestine forget about Jesus and his New Order. To ensure this oblivion for Him, they put Him to death. But He was not passive during the intrigues of the Pharisees. He held the situation in his own hand, and went to Jerusalem with a clear-eyed knowledge of the probable fate awaiting Him there. He went to establish the New Order by that act of self-sacrifice at the nation's heart. His death was at once the inauguration of the New Order and the doom of every old order which leaves Him out of account.

It is this statesmanship of Jesus which we need to study.

## I. A Statesmanlike Beginning.

It is significant that Jesus waited until He was "about thirty · years of age" before He began any public work. Years before that time He must have burned with desire to serve his people and to find his own task in the world. But He waited on at Nazareth until He was thirty years old, not, of course, because there was any magic in that particular number of years, but because the time was not ripe.

How quickly He responded when the word came to Galilee of the remarkable personality and messages of John the Baptist! All Palestine was aroused by the sensational an nouncement that the Kingdom was at hand and the equally sensational requirement of repentance in view of its nearness. Jesus immediately left the carpenter's bench and made his way to the Jordan with the multitudes. He saw in John's straightforward preaching and in the eager way in which the people of all classes responded to it exactly the conditions which made possible a wider and more lasting movement than even John contemplated. We have thought, in an earlier chapter, of the baptism and temptation of Jesus as revealing his inner experiences, but let us look at them now from the viewpoint of his statesmanship. The moral appeal · of John and the manner in which He sharpened the hopes of the people and aroused in them an eager expectancy of better things seemed to challenge Jesus to meet that widespread sense of hope and of need. He did not hesitate for a moment to make use of a tremendous popular movement which was sweeping the country. In fact, He seems to have been waiting for just such a movement before · He launched his own mission.

Then think how Jesus linked his work with John's message. We do not read far before discovering that there were wide differences between John's idea of the New Order and that held by Jesus. The principal element in the New Order as John conceived it was to be a thorough-going judgment (Mt. 3:10) and the Christ was to be a mighty Judge (Mt. 3:11, 12), but Jesus stressed service and mercy more than judgment.

Had Jesus been less of a statesman than He was, He might have felt called upon to correct these ideas and set John right at the beginning. Instead, He selected those notes in John's message which He could thoroughly approve

42

and which had already won the attention of the multitudes and began his own work by emphasizing them (Mk. 1:15). He began by discovering the large points of agreement between Himself and John and for the time ignored the points of difference. The master builder of Nazareth was constructive, and not destructive.

## II. Facing Apparent Failure.

It was natural that Jesus should begin his work in Judea. Jerusalem was the heart of the Jewish state and any reformer seeking to influence the nation would naturally begin there. It was not, then, a mark of unusual statesmanship that Jesus began his work at the nation's capital. His wisdom is revealed in the way in which He adjusted his further movements to the reception He received in Judea. For the early Judean ministry must have been judged by many to be a disappointing failure.

We may well suppose that Jesus approached the idealized religious capital of Judaism with high hopes. It stood for all the best in the nation's glorious history. In his own experience it symbolized the great spiritual awakening of his boyhood days. But He found the very temple courts where as a boy of twelve He had sat listening to the scholars transformed into a place of barter and legalized graft. And more than that, when He drove out the traders by the force of his righteous wrath, aided we may suppose by the sympathy of the people who were being fleeced and the guilty consciences of the greedy commercialists, He found Himself confronted by the religious leaders who should have been the first to come to his support. Their attitude was cold, critical, hostile. The entire incident must have been a disheartening experience for Jesus (John 2:13-22)

In addition, John tells us that the people who believed on Jesus were moved by superficial motives (2:23). And finally, as a last straw there is a hint that there was a danger of strained relations with John because of the popularity of Jesus, superficial though it was (John 4:1, 2). It is hard to imagine a more disheartening set of circumstances —opposed by the religious leaders, misunderstood by those who accepted Him and with a rivalry threatening to mar the very friendship which had made possible the beginnings of his work!

The gospels do not tell us of Jesus' heartache over Judea until the last days of his ministry, when in one passionate lament He sums up his anguish of heart, "O Jerusalem, Jerusalem! thou who murderest the prophets and stonest those who have been sent to thee! how often have I desired to gather thy children to me, just as a hen gathers her chickens under her wings, and you would not come!" (Mt. 23:37.)

But if Jesus was disappointed at the reception accorded Him in Jerusalem He did not abandon his work on that account. The real quality of his statesmanship stands revealed in the manner in which He met that rebuff. "He left Judea and departed again into Galilee" (John 4:1-3). There were other ways of gaining the ears of Palestine than by direct assault upon the nation's center.

Galilee, with its more liberal spirit, offered just the opportunity Jesus wanted. The very physical features of the country, its open, fertile fields and rolling highlands, the great international highways which passed through it, meant a more open-minded receptive people. The influence of the Pharisees was not so dominant in Galilee and something of the rigidity of Judean legalism and ceremonial was lacking there. And so, having challenged Judea in such a way as to attract the attention if not the acceptance of the capital, Jesus turned with statesmanlike acumen to the north.

## III. Popularity and Opposition.

The ministry of Jesus in Galilee is a fascinating study of practical statesmanship. It has become associated in our minds with the sermon on the mount and the parables by the sea until we fail to emphasize the consummate skill with which Jesus gauged the human forces with which He was dealing. These human forces manifested themselves in two directions, growing popularity and growing opposition. Both these movements constituted a menace to his real purposes and the genius with which He handled them will bear comparison with the highest types of political skill.

Jesus met with instant popularity in Galilee. We have only to read through the first chapter of Mark to come across such verses as, "His fame spread at once everywhere in all that part of Galilee" (vs. 28, Weymouth) and, "When they found him they said, Every one is looking for you." "Let us go elsewhere, to the neighboring country towns," He replied, "that I may proclaim my message there also" (vss. 37, 38, Weymouth); and after the healing of the leper, "The man, when he went out, began to tell every one and to publish the matter abroad, so that it was no longer possible for Jesus to go openly into any town; but he had to remain outside in unfrequented places, where people came to him from all parts" (vs. 45, Weymouth).

45

With the growing popularity came growing opposition. We shall note in another chapter Mark's summary of the development of the hostility of the religious leaders (Mk. 2-3:6). Their bitterness is traced in each stage of its development. At the healing of the paralytic borne of four (Mk. 2:1-12) their attack is spontaneous and based on high religious grounds. "Who can forgive sins but one, even God?" But in the case of the man with the withered hand (Mk. 3:1-6) their attack is deliberate, "they watched him" (vs. 2), and is based merely on traditional grounds. The climax of their attack occurs when scribes from Jerusalem (Mk. 3:22ff) assert that Jesus' motive and spirit are essentially evil. With this attack Jesus sees that the break is final and declares that an attitude which deliberately twists good into evil is unpardonable. The growth in the popular approval of Jesus comes more slowly, but we see its climax in the attempt to make Him king by force, which He avoids, withdrawing from the crowds (John 6:15).

Jesus saw both these movements and was not deceived by either of them. He knew that the crowds who came to Him were largely moved by a desire for bread or relief from physical ailments. His great heart of compassion would not let Him turn people away hungry or sick, even though He understood full well that "man shall not live by bread alone," but He was not dazzled or confused by the crowds that flocked to Him. His mission was to bring in the New Order, which meant first of all the rule of God in men's hearts, and then through them a ministry to the social needs of humanity.

A lesser leader would have thought the eager crowds spelled success. But in the very midst of this glad acceptance and enthusiasm, Jesus chose twelve men to be with him (Mk. 3:13-19). He was looking beyond this passing popularity. With the clear-eyed vision of a statesman He saw the need of a group of men, even though few in number, who should catch his spirit and interpret his message to the world.

He knew exactly what the hostility of the Pharisees meant, also. The plaudits of the crowds lulled Him into no false sense of security. These crowds would scatter with the first threatening storm, and behind the carping criticisms of the Pharisees rose the black thunder cloud of organized Judaism in all its menace and might. It was a time to test not only his courage and loyalty but also his wisdom and skill. He was not yet ready to face his foes, not because He feared them but because He dared not trust his message as yet to the few who were really beginning to share his vision of the New Order.

With marvelous insight into the situation He changed his whole method of teaching. Until the climax of the Pharisees' hostility, his teaching had been clear and definite, enlivened by many a witty allusion and illuminated by many a telling story. Now He begins to teach in parables with the express purpose of sifting his crowd (Mk. 4:12).

These parables offered nothing for the hostile Pharisees to use and they did not feed the sensational and political hopes of the crowds. They accomplished exactly what He had in mind, for Mark tells us that "when He was alone, they that were about Him with the twelve asked Him to explain the parables" (Mk. 4:10). He had succeeded in sifting the crowd and in gaining a smaller and more deeply

47

interested group, to whom He could reveal the deeper things of the New Order, its real spirit and meaning.

## IV. The Withdrawal Into the North.

The public ministry in Galilee closed with conditions which outwardly resembled the results of the early Jerusalem ministry. The religious authorities were thoroughly alienated and the crowds were dropping away. Jesus' teaching had become too deep for them. Even some of the outer circle of disciples seem to have fallen away, for after one of his most spiritual discourses we read that "many of his disciples left Him and went away, and no longer associated with Him" (John 6:66, Weymouth). But in reality the situation was quite different from those early days. When some of the disciples left Him, Jesus turned to the twelve and asked, "Will you go, too?" "Master," Simon Peter answered, "to whom shall we go? You have the words of eternal life."

He had created in that small group a loyalty upon which He could build. That splendid loyalty was the fruit of his months of labor in Galilee. Was it worth the effort? Can we think of Jesus as a statesman when He succeeded only in winning the abiding loyalty of twelve average men? And yet He entrusted the fate of the New Order to these twelve men, and although they stumbled and almost fell they did not fail Him.

With the conclusion of the public ministry in Galilee Jesus deliberately turned his back on the multitudes and withdrew into the rougher highlands of upper Galilee. There He gave Himself to the instruction of the twelve. At last came the day when He put to them the question for which

He had been preparing them all along. Mark tells the incident with his customary simplicity:

On the way He began to ask his disciples, Who do people say that I am? John the Baptist, they replied, but others say, Elijah, and others, that it is one of the prophets. Then He asked them pointedly, But you yourselves, who do you say that I am? You are the Christ, answered Peter.

That confession gains its tremendous importance in Jesus' life from the historical situation. The very circumstances in the midst of which Peter made his bold statement give it its importance. Jesus had been rejected by the church, the state and the common people. To confess Him as the leader of the New Order was to confess that the New Order itself was not the political kingdom the people expected, not the material, nationalistic kingdom of the Pharisees, but that it was a new spiritual order. In a high moment of inspiration Peter and the rest seem to have understood faintly at least the mission and the message of their Master.

They could not read that New Order in terms of the death of Jesus, however. Their very loyalty to Him blinded their eyes until they could not see how his death was to mean the ultimate victory and triumph. They could not understand how his death would reveal to them, and to all men who follow in his steps, the infinite love of God who so loved the world that He gave his only Son.

They could not understand how his death would reveal sin in all its blackness and horror and how they would come to see in the fact of Christ's Cross the double revelation of God's infinite love for humanity and of his hatred of sin. Nor could they know that his death would mean

49

release for them from their own burden of guilt and new power for living the life of the ideal citizen of the New Order. We will not censure them, for we ourselves have seen too dimly into the mystery of Jesus' death and the victory which came out of it. But patiently and repeatedly Jesus told them of the rapidly approaching crisis and what it must mean for Him (Mk. 8:31ff; 9:30ff; 10:32ff).

## V. The Last Journey to Jerusalem.

Jesus was never so truly the statesman as when "he steadfastly set his face to go to Jerusalem" (Luke 9:51). All other doors were closed. *He* had given his message in Galilee. He had won from the disciples a confession of absolute allegiance and loyalty. And He had won this confession not in an hour of personal triumph, when the crowd applauded, but in an hour of loneliness and apparent defeat. He must leave Palestine forever or face Jerusalem. And "he steadfastly set his face to go to Jerusalem." He would challenge the nation once again at its very heart. He was conscious that He went to his death. But He knew that his death meant the release of his spirit for a wider service.

"The time has come," He told certain of his disciples, "for the Son of Man to be glorified. In most solemn truth I tell you that unless the grain of wheat falls into the ground and dies, it remains what it was—a single grain; but that if it dies, it yields a rich harvest" (John 12:23, 24, Weymouth).

But in spite of his patient instruction, when the hour of his trial and death came, they could not understand. Their hearts were with Him, but Jerusalem and Rome seemed too mighty for their faith to battle against. He went to his death alone. Into that awful hour we may not go with Jesus. Who can say what the final battle meant to Him? It is enough for us that He emerged the victor from the last terrible struggle. We know that He faced death, even the death of the Cross, with a triumphant confidence that it was God's way of establishing the New Order.

With the Easter morning the statesmanship of Jesus bore amazing results. Had the little group of followers quite lost hope? If with their heads they had failed Him, were not their hearts crying out, "Who shall separate us from Christ's love? Neither death nor life!" To this group came the message of the empty tomb and the risen Lord. In a moment Jerusalem and Rome seemed powerless in comparison with the hope and the joy of the New Order which was even then beginning to be. And the spirit of the great leader who had walked with them over Galilean hills and by the Galilean lakes took command again, to send them into all the world with the transforming message of his eternal Kingdom.

# CHAPTER IV

## JESUS' IDEA OF THE NEW ORDER

### SUGGESTIONS FOR PERSONAL STUDY

**Biblical Material.**

1. Its unseen and spiritual character. Luke 17:20, 21. Contrast John 6:15 and Mk. 12:13-17.

2. Its universal scope. Mt. 8:5-13, esp. 10-12.

3. Its fundamental law. Mt. 25:31-46; Mk. 9:35; Mk. 10:35-45.

4. Its gradual growth. Mt. 13:31-33; Mk. 4:30-32; Luke 13:18, 19.

5. Its transforming effect. Luke 13:20, 21.

6. Its progressive development. Mk. 4:26-29.

7. Its inestimable value. Mt. 13:44-46.

### I. The New Order as a Kingdom.

1. Think of the New Order as the Kingdom of God. Why did Jesus use that term? Would He have used it if He had come in our day? Can you think of a better term for our use?

2. As a matter of fact, what form of government in our day best expresses the principles of the "Kingdom"? What was Jesus' characteristic name for the "King" (look through the Sermon on the Mount, Mt. 5-7, with this in view) and for the "subjects" in this Kingdom? What does this reveal concerning the New Order?

52

## II. Essentials of the New Order.

1. What is the supreme law of the New Order by which all will be impartially judged? Is that the law by which persons are estimated in your group?

2. Study Jesus' description of the great worth of the New Order. What are the values to-day for which men are willing to give all they possess? Are these values included in Jesus' Kingdom program?

3. What encouragement is to be gained from the parables of slow yet persistent growth? How are these parables at the same time a severe test for the individual and social life? What about your own growth?

4. In the light of the above questions, how would you define the New Order? Is it a thing or a spirit? Or is it a spirit seeking expression in things and among people?

We have discussed the startling effect of John's announcement that a New Order was imminent, and the way in which Jesus, far more quietly, assumed the place of leadership in this New Order. We have studied the matchless statesmanship of Jesus through the months that followed, even to the triumphant end. But why need we of the twentieth century be especially concerned about it? Is it anything more than a matter of antiquarian interest? Why bother ourselves about what took place in an outlandish corner of Syria so many centuries ago, when history is in the making so rapidly to-day?

Men dreamed of a better day long before the time of Jesus, and the air has been full of visions and hopes since

53

his time. Was his idea of the New Order so very different from these? Is it possible that the New Order He outlined will do as a program for to-day? Is it conceivable that our world is ripe for the New Order of Jesus?

Questions like these lift our study out of the realm of academic thought into contact with the rushing currents of the world's life. We must approach the problem of the New Order as Jesus shaped it with a seriousness of purpose in keeping with the earnest issues of the hour.

Some of these questions we may answer at once. There can be no possible question but that Jesus believed He was talking about something essentially different from what had gone before. Skilled teacher that He was, *H*e began where John left off, but He knew that his program was a new and radical one. He said, in defending his disciples for failure to observe certain customs, "No one ever mends an old cloak with a patch of newly woven cloth. Otherwise the patch put on would tear away some of the old, and a worse hole would be made. Nor do people pour new wine into old wineskins. Otherwise the skins would split, the wine would escape, and the skins be destroyed. But they put new wine into fresh skins and both are saved" (Mt. 9:16, 17, Weymouth). In the Sermon on the Mount He repeatedly introduced his own teaching with the remark, "You have heard that it was said to the ancients," over against which in direct contrast He sets, "But I tell you." He conceived his plan of the New Order to be very different from the Old Order. He was not a destroyer, to be sure, but a builder, and He knew that the foundations already built afforded ample base for the new structure (Mt. 5:17), but the materials were of his own choosing and He constructed it after God's plan.

The question as to whether Jesus' conception of the New Order will do for our world affords the best approach to our study of just what Jesus meant by the New Order.

## I. The New Order a Kingdom or a Democracy?

John had declared that, "the Kingdom of God is close at hand," and Jesus picked up that announcement just where John dropped it, and, sharpening the note of immediacy and adding a positive demand, He said, "The time is fully come and the Kingdom of God is close at hand; repent and believe this good news."

The term both John and Jesus used was, "the Kingdom of God." It takes conscious effort for us to speak and think of the Kingdom of God in the same clear-cut and definite way in which the people of that day used it. To them it meant not some vague and mysterious thing but a very definite state of affairs upon this earth. They differed as to the way in which the Kingdom would come but they all agreed that God would establish it upon this earth. Instead of the kingdom of Greece or Rome there would be the Kingdom of God. "And in the days of those kings shall the God of heaven set up a kingdom which shall never be destroyed.      And the kingdom shall be given to the people of the saints of the Most High" (Daniel 2:44; 7:27). Jesus meant something very different from the material, political, national kingdom of the average Jew, but his ideal was not vague or insubstantial.

But the very word *kingdom* seems to remove the idea from our world and its needs.      The passion of mankind to-day is not for another kingdom but for something to take the place of kingdoms, and even in nations ruled by kings the dominant hope is democracy. Will a New Order launched under the name of a kingdom suffice as our ideal?

It has been said that "if our Lord had come to earth to-day instead of nineteen centuries ago, He would probably have said never a word about the Kingdom of God, but would have spoken in other terms," yet "what He would have said to-day in the phrases of to-day would have had the same meaning as what He did say in the phraseology of Jewish thought." * We must look closer to discover the inner meaning of the Kingdom.

First of all, in the mind of Jesus it was the Kingdom *of God.* The absurdity and wrong of earthly kingdoms, to the mind of the average person, lie in the arbitrary elevation of one mortal man to power over his fellow mortals. But the New Order which Jesus proclaimed as "good news" was to be characterized by the extension of the rule of God, already apparent in nature, to the realm of humanity. Its very basis was in the direction of everything reasonable and right. Granted that there is a God back of the orderly and matchless processes we call nature, the only thing worth while in the world is to discover his will and accomplish it among men. But everything depends upon the kind of king God is conceived to be. If He is a tyrant the Kingdom of God will turn out to be no more endurable than any other despotism. Here we shall come to the heart of Jesus' idea of the New Order.

Look through the gospels and find the name which Jesus

* Hogg: Christ's Message of the Kingdom, page 11.

applies to God. Upon his lips the ancient terms of government and royalty are merged into those of the family. Jesus' characteristic name for God is not King but *Father* So firmly did He fix that name upon the memory of his followers that the epistles of the New Testament beauti fully speak of "the God and *Father* of our Lord Jesus Christ" (Romans 15:6). In the remarkable parable which has been called the parable of the great surprise (Mt. 25:31-46) He does use the regal title, but in such fashion as to make unmistakable the spirit of the Kingdom. It is a judgment scene in which the great King passes sentence upon all nations, but to the astonishment of those judged they are not accused or commended for their attitude toward court etiquette or royal decree but according to the manner in which they have treated the hungry, thirsty, homeless, ill-clad, sick and imprisoned. And to add to their surprise the King declares, "In solemn truth I tell you that in so far as you rendered such services to one of the humblest of these my brethren, you rendered them to me" (Mt. 25:40, Weymouth). What manner of Kingdom is this?

Jesus sharply contrasts the spirit of the Kingdom to the spirit observable in a despotism. "You are aware," He said, "how those who are deemed rulers among the Gen tiles lord it over them and their great men make them feel their authority; but it is not to be so among you. No, whoever desires to be great among you must be your servant" (Mk. 10:42, 43). Jesus did not ignore the rightful ambitions of men but He pointed out the only direction in which personal ambition can have unlimited scope in the New Order, the direction of service.

Moreover, as God is not King but *Father*, so the men

of the Kingdom are not called *subjects* but *sons,* and in their relationship to each other they are *brothers.* Jesus did not leave this side of his teaching visionary but actually created a small group of followers whom He bound into a fellowship which was the promise of this wider brother hood.

In these ways Jesus transformed the term Kingdom. By using that term He spoke to all the best in the past of the Jews but in every use of it He broadened and deepened its application until we are forced to see that He was not thinking of an archaic form of political government which a world weary of dynastic wars and social injustice is about to throw off like a worn-out cloak, but He was thinking of a *spiritual commonwealth in which a Fatherly God might express his beneficent will through brotherly men.*

Instead of the transient dream of a Galilean peasant, Jesus' New Order is a thrilling challenge to the present day.

## II. The Unseen and Spiritual Character of the New Order.

Jesus called the New Order the Kingdom of God, but we have seen that God was not a despot or the men of the Kingdom subjects or the laws of the Kingdom tyrannical decrees. All this helps us to understand the spirit of the New Order, but what of its form? Is it a republic or a democracy, is it a socialistic state or does it mean anarchy and the abolition of all government?

In our day men are mightily concerned about forms of government and we must ask what form this New Order of Jesus takes. Jesus was confronted by these same questions. There were burning political questions then as now, and by looking at his attitude toward them we may come to understand the New Order. We discover that He definitely avoided aligning the New Order with any form of political theory. Upon one occasion we read, "They were about to come and carry him off by force and make him a King, but Jesus withdrew" (John 6:15). Another time the Pharisees and Herodians, an unholy alliance, asked Him, Is it right to pay taxes to Cæsar or not? thinking, If He says yes, that will discredit Him in the eyes of all who hate Rome, and if He says no, that will involve Him in difficulties with the government. Jesus saw through the plot and we can almost see his eyes twinkle with the genuine humor of the situation as He turned to them with, "As for you Pharisees, render to Cæsar the things that are Cæsar's, and as for you Herodians, render to God the things that are God's" (cf. Mk. 12:13-15).

Apparently He would not commit the New Order to any outward form of government. From one point of view this just suited the Pharisees, for they thought it impossible to throw off the Roman yoke. Their ideas of the Kingdom were strictly materialistic and national, however, for they expected the Kingdom to come down out of the heavens, by the miraculous act of God, and then to be established upon earth for Jews and Jews only, and they were always speculating about the signs and portents which should announce its coming. But Jesus seems to have refused just as definitely to align his New Order with their idea.

It is in contrast to the Pharisees' conception of the new order that Jesus made the most illuminating statement to be found anywhere in the gospels concerning his conception of the Kingdom. They had asked about its coming and apparently some were saying, It will come in this form, and others, It will come in that form, and then they came to Jesus with the question, What form do you think the Kingdom will take? Jesus answered, The Kingdom of God will not be a form at all, and when you get this form of government or that order of political theory you won't be able to say, Behold here the Kingdom is or there it is, for the Kingdom of God is not a form of government, it is an inner spirit; the Kingdom of God is within you (Luke 17:20, 21). In essence the New Order is unseen and spiritual. It works its way from the inside out and not from the outside in.

This is not to say that Jesus' New Order is an intangible something, and that if He were here in human form to-day He would not be passionately interested in the rising tide of democracy in our world; it is simply to say that He did not commit the Kingdom to any political organization but that He did believe that the spirit of brotherhood in the hearts of his followers would create the type of government best suited to the expression of itself.

*The New Order is an unseen and spiritual commonwealth seeking to create in the world appropriate political and social forms for its adequate expression.*

## III. Characteristics of the New Order.

Jesus illustrated the characteristics of the New Order by the use of a wealth of figures and parables, each one of which adds to the picture as a whole. The symbols He used in describing the Kingdom are significant, in that they are the common and ever present realities of life. The words most frequently upon his lips are such terms as light, heaven, salt, seed, living water. He sought to convey in terms of the common life his great spiritual message. He was a true artist, not simply because of the rhetorical fitness and beauty of the symbols He chose, but because these symbols give us an insight into the inner meaning of the truth they are meant to convey.

In speaking of the *inestimable value* of the New Order He said, it is like "treasure buried in the open country which a man finds, but buries again, and in his joy about it goes and sells all he has and buys that piece of ground," and similarly, it is like "a jewel merchant who is in quest of choice pearls. He finds one most costly pearl; he goes away; and though it costs all he has, he buys it" (Mt. 13: 44-46, Weymouth). These vivid parables seem to illustrate but one phase of the New Order, its priceless value, but the figures most frequently used set forth the New Order as a living, moving thing. How perfectly Jesus describes the *gradual growth* of the Kingdom, in the parables of the mustard seed (Mt. 13:31, 32), the developing grain (Mk. 4:26-29), the wheat and tares! (Mt. 13:24-30.)

Could a more telling vehicle for teaching the *transforming effect,* gradual yet persistent, of the Kingdom spirit be conceived than the parable of the yeast? "To what shall I compare the Kingdom of God? It is like yeast which a woman takes and buries in a bushel of flour, to work there till the whole is leavened" (Luke 13:21, Weymouth). The New Order works quietly like the yeast. It persists until the whole is leavened. Just as the mass of dough rising and falling, the bubbles swelling and bursting, are only a proof of the active presence of the yeast, so the troubled surface of human history reveals the presence of the truth of God at work in the world, and we may take heart from the very upheavals of humanity. And the New Order, like the yeast, works by contagion. The yeast, insignificant in quantity compared with the mass of dough,· could never pervade the whole except that each tiny particle of leaven communicates itself to those particles nearest it. Similarly by contagion of character the New Order finds its growth.

These parables of growth seem to suggest that the coming of the New Order depends upon the *co-operation of men with God.* As it is God whose earth and air and sunshine mature and foster the seed, so it is man whose planting and tending must render the gifts of God operative in human conditions. But even while realizing this responsibility, man need not be anxious for the fruitage, for that is in God's own hands· "The earth bears fruit of itself; first the blade, then the ear, then the full grain in the ear" (Mk. 4:26-29). Jesus fully describes the part human effort will play in the coming of the New Order and this must be our study in a later chapter.

Finally Jesus' characterization of the New Order lifted it out of its national and materialistic limitations into the realm of a universal commonwealth of the spirit. This appears almost as strikingly from his silences as from his utterances, for He has nothing to say about Rome or the overthrow of Israel's enemies or her triumphant rule. "What He has to say does not concern men as Jews but men as men." * Upon one occasion particularly, when the faith of a Roman captain was revealed, He solemnly declared in a memorable figure, "I tell you that many will come from the east and from the west and will recline at the table with Abraham,

* Rall: New Testament History, p. 70.

Isaac and Jacob in the Kingdom of the heavens, while the natural heirs of the Kingdom will be driven out into the darkness outside" (Mt. 8:10-12)

## IV. The New Order an Individual and Social Reality.

We have emphasized the New Order as something which is first of all, inner and spiritual, but we suggested that Jesus' idea was no less concrete than the current conceptions, even though his Kingdom is neither nationalistic nor materialistic. It is very easy for us to volatilize the New Order of Jesus into a series of abstractions, but if it was only an impracticable dream it will not do for our day. It is a doubtful gain to see a fairer vision if the new be as unattainable as the old. Such a vision only brings added despair to a world eager for help.

In reality, the supreme contribution of Jesus to our world was his own life, lived under conditions such as we have to face, for He not only had to preach about the New Order but He lived it. When there appeared upon the plains of human history One whose faith in God was unwavering and unbroken, the Kingdom became a concrete reality. Jesus moved about supplementing at every turn weak and defective human life. He proved in terms of deeds, which are their own best commentary, that God has no joy in sin and suffering and disease, in human hunger and want and ignorance. He embodied the Kingdom spirit. In Him the New Order became a living reality.

He did more than that. He gathered about Him a dozen ordinary men whom no one could accuse of being saints or philosophers, and by means of that little group He made the Kingdom a social reality. It was a slow process, imperfectly realized, yet at the end He had so lived Himself into their lives that He could commit the entire future of the New Order to them, and all that is best and finest in our civilization we owe to the fact that in those twelve men the Kingdom became a social fact.

Throughout the succeeding ages this inner spiritual Kingdom has sought social expression. Often the social expression has been utterly inadequate; always it has needed to be corrected by the Master who called it into being. And never before in all history has the world been in such dire need of adequate expression, through a human brotherhood, of the Kingdom spirit of the Christ.

## V. A Summary.

Jesus' idea of the New Order, then, is the reign of a Fatherly God in the hearts of men who thereby become brothers. Its fundamental law is the law of service. While primarily a matter of the spirit and never to be confused with outward forms of government or theological speculation, this New Order seeks adequate social and political forms of expression, in every age. It is of inestimable value, worthy of the entire resources of the individual, a thing of slow growth but of transforming power. While it challenges the highest idealism, it has actually been realized upon our earth and is capable of successful approximation by common men. It is the Supreme Good of human existence, carrying with it in proper relationship all other things of real worth (Mt. 6:33).

How we may qualify for citizenship in this New Order will be our next study.

# CHAPTER V

## CONDITIONS OF ENTRANCE

### SUGGESTIONS FOR PERSONAL STUDY

**Biblical Material.**

1. Repentance and belief. Mk. 1:15.

2. Following Jesus. Mk. 1:16-20 cf. Mt. 4:18-22 and Luke 5:1-11; Mk. 2:13, 14.

3. Appreciation. Luke 14:15-24.

4. Receptivity. Mk. 10:13-16 cf. Mt. 19:13-15 and Luke 18:15-17.

5. Warning notes.

    a. The danger of riches. Mk. 10:17-27 cf. Mt. 19:16-26 and Luke 18:18-27.

    b. Sacrifice of personal considerations. Mk. 9:43-47 cf. Mt. 5:29, 30.

    c. The cost. Luke 14:25-33 cf. Mt. 10:37, 38.

    d. The demands. Luke 9:57-62 cf. Mt. 8:19-22.

6. Individual cases.

    a. The fishermen and Matthew. Mk. 1:16-20; 2:13, 14.

    b. The Gerasene demoniac. Mk. 5:18-20 esp. vs. 19.

    c. Zaccheus. Luke 19:1-10.

    d. The rich young man. Mt. 19:16-20.

7. A transformed life. John 3:1-3.

## THE WAY OF CHRIST

### I. Positive Demands.

1. Try to frame the positive requirements of Jesus in the terms of life to-day. What is repentance in view of the coming of the New Order? Does it refer to something more than mere "personal" wrong doing? Does it include one's attitude to one's group? Does it include negligence and a lack of responsibility as well as positive social sins?

2. What does it mean to "believe" in the New Order? How would you distinguish "belief" from "hope" in regard to the coming of a New Order? Is your attitude one of "hope" or "belief"?

3. Examine the statement, "Follow me." What did it mean for the fishermen and Matthew? Does it mean anything so radical as that now?

4. Study "appreciation" and "receptivity" as Kingdom qualities. What is the importance of these qualities in ordinary social life? Are they equally applicable to the New Social Order and to one's attitude toward truth?

### II. Hindrances.

1. Read over these hindrances as Jesus sets them forth, materialism, selfishness, superficial enthusiasm (failure to count the cost), etc. Add to the list present-day hindrances to citizenship in the New Order. What are your personal hindrances?

### III. The Transformed Life.

1. Note the variety of circumstances under which the men whom Jesus transformed spent their lives.

2 Can you see an answer to Nicodemus' question (John

3:4) in the transformation wrought in the lives of Zaccheus and others.?

3. What has the leadership of Jesus meant in your life? Is it because of failure to meet his demands that it has not meant more?

In the last chapter we sought to define the New Order as it appears in Jesus' teaching. Now we are going to see it as Jesus presents it to the men of his own day, in its claims upon them and its relation to the lives they were living. We shall come to closer grips with the New Order in this connection, for this was Jesus' way of presenting it. He never defined the Kingdom and seems not to have been greatly concerned about theories, but He was concerned about people. Practically everything He said was the product of the give-and-take of personal conversation or of some concrete human situation. A wayside encounter, a quiet noontide talk, the action of religious leaders, the needs of a crowd, these called forth his most profound words.

In our day we are challenged to remember that this Jesus, whom we have sometimes been tempted to think of as a dreamer, did not outline his splendid ideal of a New Order in the quiet of a hermit's cell or a scholar's study. In fact, He never committed a word of it to writing. It was all the product of face-to-face contact with living men and women in the midst of the rough and tumble of life. For these reasons the New Order gains in reality when we see how Jesus put it up to ordinary men.

Any movement or organization stands revealed by its requirements even more than by its promises or ideals. We shall be able to put the New Order to this practical test by asking what the conditions of entrance are as Jesus formulated them. The answer will be found under four general statements. First, the conditions of entrance into the New Order are very simple. Second, they are very exacting. Third, they differ with different individuals. Fourth, participation in the New Order means a transformed person.

## I. The Simplicity of the Conditions.

When we remember that Jesus is here beginning the proclamation of a world religion which has lasted through nineteen centuries and has claimed the allegiance of the most progressive nations and races of the world, the naked simplicity of his initial demands upon men is astounding. He began by announcing, "The time has fully come, and the Kingdom of God is close at hand: repent and believe this Good News" (Mk. 1:15, Weymouth). Some time after this He was passing along the shore of the Lake of Galilee and saw there two pairs of brothers, fishermen, and He said to them, "Come and follow me" (Mk. 1:16), and they left their nets and followed him. Another incident, later in his ministry, is characteristic of the demands He made. "They were bringing little children to Jesus, that he might touch them; but the disciples rebuked them. But when Jesus saw it, he was indignant, and said to them, Let the little children come to me and forbid them not; *for of such is the Kingdom of God.* I tell you truly, Whoever shall not receive the Kingdom of God as a little child, shall by no means enter it" (Mk. 10:13-16).

Again He told of a man who planned to give a great

68

supper and invited many people. But when the time for the supper arrived, with ludicrous unanimity they pleaded pressing engagements. Then the master of the house said to his servant, "If these people don't want to eat my supper I will invite people who do. Go out quickly into the streets and lanes of the city, and bring in here the poor and the cripples, the blind and the lame." And the master of the house added, "I tell you not one of those men who were invited shall taste of my supper" (Luke 14:15-24).

Could anything be easier or simpler? He demanded the same genuine repentance which had been John's keynote. He insisted that people have a thoroughly positive attitude toward the good news that the New Order was at hand. They must believe it and they must be willing to show the genuineness of their belief by readjusting their lives to the extent of literally following Him if He demanded it. They must have the teachableness of a child and they must be hungry for the New Order. *Repent, Believe in the Good News, Follow Me, Be Teachable, Be Hungry for the New Order.* These are the characteristic demands which Jesus made in the early days in Galilee.

Jesus asked for a certain attitude rather than any attainment. The men whom He called into fellowship with Himself were not versed in theology. They had no well-defined theory about Jesus. They were not asked to confess any creed. He did not demand perfection of character or an adequate intellectual grasp of the Kingdom. As a matter of fact, long after this these men were both unstable in character and clouded in understanding. They were not saints or theologians, but they were men of moral earnestness, who were ready to commit their lives to the New Order, and they were so hungry and thirsty for the righteousness that should characterize it, that in true teachableness and humility they left all and followed Jesus.

Are these the initial conditions of entrance into the New Order to-day? If Jesus were to walk among men to-day would He attach unto Himself the men and the women who are hungry and thirsty for justice and mercy in our world, who are willing to commit themselves body and soul to the better day? Just what tests would He apply now?

## II. The Exacting Demands of the New Order.

The exacting nature of Jesus' demands are even more astounding than their simplicity. Each one of the simple conditions for entrance into the New Order is rigorously thorough-going. Jesus meant by *Repent* just that moral renovation of the entire life which John the Baptist had called for. He meant by *Believe in the Good News* no saccharine optimism that "things will come out right in the end," but a *personal commitment* to the New Order. *Belief* such as He called for was not an uncertain step in the dark but the launching of the entire personality in the service of the Kingdom. And when He said, *Follow me,* He made the most severe demand of all.

We have thought often of the beauty of that scene by Galilee (Mk. 1:16-20). The fishermen are at their nets; the strolling Teacher passes by; He calls them into pleasant fellowship with Him, and they leave their boats and the blue waters of Galilee. But the dominant note of the picture is power. Jesus is taking control of the lives of these men. He is asking no less than that they abandon their life tasks and at his bidding undertake an entirely new

70

adventure. This is something radical. And then his requirement that citizens of the New Order have the child like spirit, that seems harmless enough! "The Kingdom of God belongs to those who are childlike" (Mk. 10:14). But we need to remember that in this same connection He said: "In solemn truth I tell you that no one who does not receive the Kingdom of God like a little child will by any possibility enter it" (Mk. 10:15). And even the genuinely humorous and delightful story of the man who gave the great supper (Luke 14:15-24) concludes with a grave warning: "For I tell you, not one of those men who were invited shall taste of my supper."

We do not have to read far in the gospels to discover how serious the matter of citizenship in the New Order really is. Jesus' demands were exactly as uncompromising as the demands which a nation makes of her citizens in time of war. He said: "If any one is coming to me who does not hate his father and mother, wife and children, brothers and sisters, yes and his own life also, he cannot be a disciple of mine" (Luke 14:26, 27). We used to find it necessary to explain that Jesus' words were hyperbolic, and that He was only demanding that absolute loyalty which will be ready to break all home ties, but millions have learned by experience just what Jesus meant by the partings that seem little less cruel than hate.

In similar passages (Luke 9:57-62) Jesus emphasized absolute loyalty as a requirement of the New Order. His words, "No man who looks back after having put his hand to the plow is fit for the Kingdom of God," are still the classic expression of unswerving loyalty to a cause. He needed heroic men who were ready to sacrifice all and venture all.

Yet He asked his disciples to sit down first and with absolute sincerity to count the cost (Luke 14:28-33).

By means of startling figures of speech, Jesus taught that all personal considerations, however dear or indispensable they seem, must be sacrificed for the New Order. "If your hand should cause you to sin, cut it off; it would be better for you to enter into life maimed," etc. (Mk. 9:43-47, Weymouth). And to the amazement of his disciples He re peatedly declared that wealth was often a barrier to citi zenship in the New Order, and in particular cases where it was evidently such a barrier He did not hesitate to advise that it be disposed of (Mk. 10:17-27)

### III. Readjustments in the Lives of Individuals. 

We have reviewed the simple yet exacting conditions of entrance into the New Order. In general Jesus called for a whole-hearted loyalty to the Kingdom. But He did not set forth any *one* way in which that loyalty must find expression, and, as a matter of fact, we find a variety of individual readjustments caused by allegiance to the New Order.

For twelve men, citizenship in the New Order meant leaving their fishing boats (Mk. 1:16-20) and their business offices (Mk. 2:13, 14) to follow Jesus. Mark's gospel, with characteristic conciseness, explains the purpose of this summons: "He appointed twelve that they might be with him and that he might send them forth" (Mk. 3:14). Throughout the Christian centuries "*Following Christ*" has meant just such a radical change in the entire circumstances of groups of men, and with the same end in view, "that they might be with him and that he might send them forth." The manifold ministries of the modern church and the richly varied opportunities of the missionary field repeat Christ's words, "Come and follow me," and for many, citizenship can mean no less than dropping everything to respond.

But although the pages of our records are largely filled with the doings of Jesus and these twelve whom He called into fellowship, there are not wanting priceless accounts of what happened in the lives of certain common men who were not asked to leave all and follow Him.

One such individual wanted to give up everything else and follow Jesus, but Jesus very definitely told him that citizenship in his case meant something more prosaic, if just as serviceable. Read the dramatic story of the insane man of the Gerasene country (Mk. 5:1-20 and parallels). This wild man of the hills had terrorized the whole country-side, but the quiet majesty of the Master was more than a match for his untamed spirit and he found himself restored to that world from which he had been cut off. Imagine his relief and joy! It does him no little credit that as the Master is about to leave he rushes up to the boat and with heart swelling with gratitude cries out, "Take me with you, I'll serve you, I'll go anywhere with you. Only take me with you." But Jesus turns to him with the answer, "No. Go home to your friends and tell them what the Lord has done for you and how he has had mercy on you."

It was not an easy commission. One can imagine that in the home community the man restored to sanity would meet some suspicion. Neighbor would remark to neighbor, "I understand that So-and-so is home again, and they say he is clothed and in his right mind. But as for me" (with a shrug of the shoulder) "I think he will bear watching. You never can tell about people that have had that disease."

Far more romantic would have been the companionship with Jesus in strange regions. But citizenship for him meant taking his religion home with him and living it out under familiar and prosaic circumstances. And he did it, with what results the gospel story records. His transformed life was a telling sermon to the entire district (Mk. 5:20).

Like Kipling's Mulholland we are prone to want to preach our religion "handsome and out of the wet," but "The word of the Lord were lain upon me, and I done what I was set."

Luke has preserved for us the story of a man for whom entrance into the Kingdom meant a readjustment of his business practices (Luke 19:1-10). No character in the New Testament has more of human interest than this same Zaccheus. Here as ever Luke is the artist, and with a few deft strokes of the pen he lets us see and understand his character. "He was a chief publican and he was rich." This man had money but no friends. To all Jericho this tax gatherer was a renegade Jew who had sold his country for pieces of silver. He had his fine house but no friends. No wonder the publicans became a lot of cynical, sour, hard-hearted, tight-fisted men! But this Zaccheus had higher aspirations than his kind. He had heard of a man gifted beyond belief with a genius for friendship, and when the report came that Jesus was drawing near to Jericho, Zaccheus was in the crowd. It is a humorous yet pathetic picture Luke gives us of the little man who overcame the handicap of his stature by climbing the mulberry tree. How the crowd must have appreciated the joke of this rich official "up a tree!"

And then Jesus came. He took in the situation at a glance.

74

About Him a crowd of the curious, the sensation-loving, and there in the tree the little man hungry for friendship. If there had been a touch of the demagogue about Jesus, what a roar of laughter and applause He could have drawn from the crowd by some witty sally about the unpopular Zaccheus! But instead, with fine courage, He looked up at him and said, "Zaccheus, come down quickly, for I must stay at your house to-day." With eager and joyous haste the publican scrambles down and leads Jesus away to his home to be his guest! But as they move through the streets of the city he hears the comments of the accompanying throng. "Aha," they are saying, "so *He* has gone in to be the guest of a notorious sinner! Can you see the flush rise on Zaccheus' cheek? And now they come to his home and Jesus is about to enter when, at the very threshold, Zaccheus pauses, and half facing the Lord and half facing the crowd he declares, "Here and now, Master, I give half my property to the poor, and if I have unjustly exacted money from any man, I pledge myself to repay to him four times the amount." Turning to him, Jesus replied, "To-day salvation has come to this house" (Weymouth). These were the conditions of entrance into the New Order which Zaccheus and many of his kind have to face.

One more candidate for citizenship in the New Order— and this is the finest type of all (Mk. 10:17-22). There came running to Jesus a young man. He did not bear the marks of a misspent life or of a crooked and wasted character. He came rather all unexhausted in his potentialities and powers. And Jesus, Mark tells us, looking upon him, loved him, for his youth, for his moral rectitude, for his unsullied physique, for the clean-cut, clear-eyed strength

75

and purity of his character. And this youth said, "Respected Teacher, what is your rule for life? I have learned and observed the program of my religion but I am not satisfied." And Jesus replied, "You don't need another rule or another law. You have had ethical programs enough. Don't think of me just as a *Good Teacher* but cut adrift from your wealth and *follow* me. Your need is for God. Come with me and learn of Him." And the youth turned away, for he had great wealth.

He thought his need was for another precept, a shorter, more satisfying intellectual statement. But Jesus knew that his need was for inner power. If he followed Jesus he must have been led where all the rest were led, into the consciousness of God's presence in his life. For Jesus led men into the presence of God so that they could call Him Father and understand his will and receive strength to do it long before they were intellectually able to explain all their experiences.

Are there those whose need now is a like simplicity of guidance even in the face of unsolved intellectual and ethical tangles? Does citizenship to-day mean cutting adrift from entangling hindrances of every sort?

## IV. A Transformed Person.

Now there was one of the Pharisees whose name was Nicodemus, a ruler among the Jews. He came to Jesus by night and said, Rabbi, we know that you are a teacher come from God; for no one can do these miracles which you are doing, unless God is with him.

In most solemn truth I tell you, answered Jesus, that unless a man is born anew he cannot see the Kingdom of

God. . . . How is all this possible? asked Nicodemus (John 3:1-3, Weymouth).

These words have seemed to every generation of Christians through all the centuries to be the most adequate and fitting description of entrance into the Kingdom of God. The wonder, the mystery, the joy, the newness of physical birth symbolize the renewal of life which citizenship in the New Order means. How is all this possible? Nicodemus asked, and Jesus replied that it could not be explained like a problem in mathematics; it is above earthly things (John 3:12). And yet, think of these men we have been studying, so different one from another, the rich young ruler, the successful business man, the poor weak-minded Gerasene, some fishermen and tradesmen, as widely different as men are to-day. Was it anything less than a new birth for Zachcheus, when he shook off the crooked practices of a business lifetime and courageously faced his sneering neighbors? He had become a new man. And the restored demoniac, was he not proving the birth of a new life within when he set his face back to the prosaic life of the home community? As for Zaccheus, it had all come about through his hunger for a friend and his sincere welcoming of Jesus not only to his home but into the inner household of his heart. As for the fishermen, the miracle happened because they followed Jesus. As for Paul, he, too, saw Jesus and confessed Him as the leader of the New Order, and the miracle was wrought in his life. It is Paul who has given this new birth its classic expression: "It is no longer I that live, but Christ that liveth in me."

And so through all the centuries as men have followed

Jesus the new life has come into being. Our study of the varied experiences of these varied men will teach us to look for the new life in no stereotyped way, at no set times or seasons, but we will confidently expect it wherever men follow Jesus.

O holy Child of Bethlehem, descend to us, we pray,
Cast out our sin and enter in, be born in us to-day.

# CHAPTER VI

## THE IDEAL CITIZEN

### SUGGESTIONS FOR PERSONAL STUDY

**Biblical Material.**
1. The ideal citizen. Mt. 5:1-12.
2. His two-fold responsibilities. Mt. 5:13-16.
3. The danger of misdirecting his energies. Mt. 5:38-48.

**I. The Ideal Citizen.**

1. Paraphrase the Beatitudes (Mt. 5:1-12), substituting for the biblical phrases modern terms which express what you think Jesus meant.

2. Try to form a picture of a person embodying all the characteristics of the ideal citizen. Would such a person be a positive or a negative character? Which characteristics seem negative? Which are unquestionably positive? If certain characteristics seem negative try thinking of them with reference to the New Order. For example, would mourning at the triumph of evil be possible for a strong character?

3. Think again about the ideal citizen in the light of the above questions. If such a person were to appear in your community or group what would be the result? What person in the circle of your acquaintances is nearest to this ideal? Is that person a positive or a negative individual?

II. **The Twofold Responsibilities of the Ideal Citizen.**
Mt. 5:13-16.

1. Study these two figures of speech. What kind of a force is the citizen of the New Order to be? What do you mean when you say of a person, "He's the salt of the earth?"

2. In what sense do these words of Jesus constitute a challenge? In what sense are they a warning? Would these words seem to imply that if one is actually a citizen of Jesus' New Order he must "save" and "shine"?

III. **Misdirected Energies.** Mt. 5:38-48.

1. What is the main idea in these perplexing illustrations? Who is it that is in danger of being injured in each case?

2. As a matter of practical experience how much satisfaction have you had from any attempts to avenge insults and injuries? How many friends have you made in that way?

3. Is Jesus' teaching here about misdirected and selfishly directed energies capable of a wider application than to individuals? Is it applicable to nations?

Try to formulate again your picture of the ideal citizen of the New Order.

Power attracts every normal person.

Who has not felt a sense of satisfaction as inch by inch, foot by foot, the driving, steady, undaunted force within the automobile eats up a long steep hill? It is the satisfaction of power, a sense of union and fellow feeling with the engine, an exaltation as from a personal triumph. Or remember the great power house with its low, dull hum of ponderous machines, perfectly adjusted, nicely oiled, the caldron where is brewed so much of the magic of modern life.

We see more than revolving wheels and clever mechanism. We see a whole network of transportation facilities and tens of thousands of gleaming lights, and we pay our tribute to the genius of the inventor and the accuracy and patience and skill of the mechanic. But it is the great something which genius and skill and accuracy and patience, coöperating, have discovered and harnessed that enthralls us. It is the power that fascinates.

Power attracts every normal person whether manifested in a great waterfall, a mighty locomotive or a dynamic human personality. Shakespeare's Julius Cæsar had his weaknesses. He was deaf in one ear, a poor judge of character, and eaten up with ambition. But in spite of all the defects which history can discover or fiction invent, this man made his impress on the world's life, and rulers have delighted in the titles Czar and Kaiser because of the power of one Cæsar.

While strength and ambition are ours, we all share this thirst for power. Not that we would wield the influence of a Cæsar, but that we would have an abundant life, full and rich. We are not content to think of ourselves as mere pawns in the cosmic game or cogs in a great machine. Any philosophy or religion which would win our allegiance must promise an enlarging, more abundant, more powerful life.

Surely this is the characteristic demand which our age makes of Christianity. It must offer this richer, more satisfying, and particularly this more potent life. Our query in this chapter will be, What kind of person is the ideal citizen of Jesus' New Order?˙ We must ask frankly if he is actually a satisfying ideal for us to-day.

## I. Our Ideal Citizen.

"As one reads the Gospels there meet him two great words which announce the nature of the teaching. . . . The first is the word Power, the second is the word Life."* "The Christian," says the author of "Ecce Homo," "has passed from passive to active humanity."

Quotations such as the above suit our modern thought about the Christian. We like to think that there is nothing negative about him. He is masculine and potent, a maximum personality, bubbling over with energy and enthusiasm. He incorporates all the most aggressive qualities of our modern business heroes. Just as the engineer "belts on to cosmic forces, harnesses his machinery to the lightnings and runs the earth at the impulse of the sky and the spaces," so the Christian has "belted on" to the invisible spiritual forces of our universe until, as we put it, he "does things."

Our ideal is the active, positive Christian, a force in the world. The business of the Christian, as Dr. Parkhurst once put it, is "to prove to the world that people who sniff at a religion that runs over with God and celestial energy are as slow and as far in the rear of their opportunities as would be the man who should transport freight from New York to Chicago on a donkey cart or carry American tourists to Europe in a row boat." Our ideal citizen is up-to-date.

Moreover, he is robustly athletic. No pale-faced ascetic will satisfy us. He must have nerves, prompt and accurate

* Peabody: The Christian Life in the Modern World, p. 32.

as telegraph instruments, a heart action which is reliable and efficient, lungs which are sound, muscles ready to tackle hard work and laugh at it. He will rejoice in the "game" of life. We have revised our picture of the young man Jesus Christ because only a magnificent physique seems the proper bodying forth of that magnificent spirit.

Our ideal Christian, then, has the aggressiveness of a successful business man, the efficiency of an engineer, the mental alertness of the trained thinker, the physique of an athlete, the courage, discipline and endurance of a soldier. He is a composite of our present-day heroes. There is something behind and beneath all these characteristics, of course, which is the reason why we call him a *Christian*. But do we not hope that Jesus' ideal citizen will turn out to be just such a positive, successful, satisfying person as we have been thinking about?

## II. Jesus' Ideal Citizen.

Happy the poor in spirit!
*For* theirs is the Kingdom of Heaven.
Happy the meek!
*For* they shall inherit the earth.
Happy they who mourn!
For they shall be comforted.
*H*appy they who hunger and thirst for righteousness!
For they shall be satisfied.
Happy the merciful!
For they shall obtain mercy.
*H*appy the pure in heart!
For they shall see God.
*H*appy the peacemakers!
For they shall be called sons of God.

Happy they who have been persecuted on account of righteousness!

For theirs is the Kingdom of Heaven.

Happy are you when men shall denounce you and persecute you,

Speaking falsely on account of me, and denounce and persecute and say all manner of evil against you!

Rejoice and exult! For great is your reward in heaven.

For so they persecuted the prophets who were before you. (Mt. 5:3-12, translation from Kent: Life and Teachings of Jesus, p. 204.)

. We read these words with a sense of bewilderment. Did Jesus throw open the doors of the New Order to the poor in spirit, the meek, the mournful, the merciful? Are the peacemaker and the persecuted his ideal? Involuntarily we say these are all negative qualities. They describe a good saint but not a good citizen. We repeat these famous Beatitudes with mental reservations because somehow they fail to hit off the needs of our life. Can we set an ideal like that before the young manhood and womanhood of our world? It seems far from a positive picture of the Christian life. This might do for a little group of saints, who needed the assurance of future rewards as they faced persecution; our own need is for a positive program for this world.

But before we turn from the Beatitudes as a hopelessly negative portrayal of an ideal person, we need to think more carefully about them. In the first place we need to remember that the author of these words was no negative personality. He set in motion forces which have come sweeping down through the centuries. Indeed, a strong case can be made out for the proposition that Jesus Christ deliberately chose such forceful ways for presenting his claims and the claims of the Kingdom that the world could not ignore or forget them.

Moreover, as a great scholar has finely put it, in these Beatitudes, "it is not so much a question of recompense as of consequence" (Plummer). When Jesus said, Happy the meek, for they shall inherit the earth, He was not assigning an arbitrary future reward, but announcing a great spiritual law, namely, that meekness actually results in such an inherit ance. At any rate, happiness is declared to be the present possession of the person who bears these characteristics.

And finally, we need to remember that positiveness is not the same thing as bluster. The most powerful forces in our world move quietly. Let us think, then, about this ideal citizen as Jesus pictures him, to see if he really is a negative person.

### III. A Positive or a Negative Person?

What if the "poor in spirit" are not the physically and morally anemic, but those men and women who feel as the deepest need of their lives the presence and power of God's reinforcing spirit, who face their tasks with a sense of utter dependence upon Him, who would fain enrich their own spiritual poverty from the exhaustless treasuries of God? Who were the people in the Palestine of Jesus' day whom He could not touch or influence? Not the ignorant or the morally perverted but the self-sufficient, who, encased in the armor of their spiritual satisfaction, were impervious alike to the love and the power of the Master. Is that what Jesus meant in the parable of the Pharisee and the Publican? Was the publican "poor in spirit"? (Luke 18:9-14.)

## THE WAY OF CHRIST

What if "the meek" are not the mollycoddles, but those strong men and women who know that humility is the level where we must all stand if we would learn and the garment we must all wear if we would work. Have we false conceptions of meekness because of the people who have thought it could be gained by direct assault? who have said, Go to now, I will be humble? who have arrived at a spurious humility strangely like pride? Humility is attained by looking up and out, not in,—up at God's standards and out upon humanity's needs.

When men really pray, humility is there. It was only the Master who could say, "I am meek and lowly." Paul said, "I am the least of the apostles," but he hastened to add, "I labored more abundantly than they all." That is the test of genuine humility. We must beware of the meekness which says, "I can be humble and lowly but I can't do anything," for meekness is not an end but an atmosphere. Let no one say, "I am the least" unless he is willing to add, "Therefore I will work twice as hard," for the necessity which humility imposes is "labors more abundant." Humility and labors more abundant form a tremendous, an almost irresistible combination.

What if they who "mourn" are not the sad-faced, gloomy pessimists of life, upset by trivial misfortunes and slight personal inconveniences, but rather those whose deepest desires are to see the New Order realized here and now and who are cut to the quick by every triumph of evil. Is it right to say that the only sorrow and grief which is in harmony with God's will is the heartache at the delay in the coming of his Kingdom in which all suffering and sorrow will vanish?

Are not "mourners" of this sort the only people who can be righteously and permanently happy?

What if this ideal citizen is filled with a divine discontent at his own spiritual attainment (Mt. 5:4) is mastered by an intense longing for God's forgiveness and approval (v. 6), becomes the harmony-maker or whole-maker of his community (v. 9) and persists in such a program in spite of all discouragements (v. 10, 11)?

Imagine what would happen in your community if there should appear such an individual, a true citizen of the New Order, utterly dependent upon God for strength, hungering and thirsting for righteousness in the common life, cut to the quick by every blasting influence which threatens, a champion of wholesomeness in social relationships (v. 9), self-forgetful in service, pure of heart, compassionate, and filled with that deep and permanent joy which is the keynote of the New Order. Would you think of him as a negative personality or the most powerful and positive influence in your group?

## IV. The Nature of the Force Which the Citizen Exerts.

As though He were speaking to our modern perplexity Jesus goes on to describe the nature of the power which the ideal citizen is to exert.

"You are the salt of the earth; but if salt has become tasteless, in what way can it regain its saltness? It is no longer good for anything but to be thrown away and trodden on by the passers by. You are the light of the world; a town cannot be hid if built on a hill-top. Nor is a lamp lighted to be put under a bushel, but on a lamp-stand; and then it gives light to all in the house. Just so let your light shine before all men, in order that they may see your holy lives and give glory to your Father who is in Heaven." (Mt. 5:13-16, Weymouth.)

There can be no possible mistake here. The citizen of the Kingdom is to be a positive force. Can you think in all the world of forces, of any two which are more humble, less boisterous, farther removed from bluster, than salt and sunshine? And can you think of any two which are more powerful, more wholesome? Pliny said, "There is nothing more useful than salt and sunshine." The citizen of the New Order is to be both.

How personal Jesus made this statement! He plainly said, *You* are the light and the salt. *We* have been saying, *Christianity* is the light and the salt, as though there were abroad in the world a vague, undefined force, disassociated from people so commonplace as Smith and Brown and Jones. We thanked God for our Christian civilization and Christian influences. And then a great flood of war engulfed the world and we looked in vain for Christian civilization and influence to assert its impersonal power and stop the war. But is there any such thing as Christianity apart from persons? And has not this war brought to each of us a sense of shame and sorrow as we confess that the light of Christ has been rather *shining upon* us than *burning in us?* It has been *preserving us,* and not in us as a *saving power* for society.*

The positive character of the citizen and the nature of the force he is to exert are brought to further clearness in those

* Hogg: Christ's Message of the Kingdom, p. 4.

perplexing illustrations about the way to deal with personal insults. Jesus seems to give no place for that hot pride and revengeful spirit which flares up unbidden at the slap on the cheek (Mt. 5:39) or the more studied wrong-doing (v. 40) or the restriction of personal liberty (v. 41). Can Jesus have meant us to take a negative attitude toward the wickedness of bad men? Impossible! we say. His whole life is the answer to that, for He did more to vanquish evil than any one who ever lived.

This novel method of dealing with personal insults must be, in Jesus' thought, the strongest way of fighting evil. Perhaps He was trying to direct the positive efforts of the citizen into constructive channels. How much of our energy is spent in worrying about whether we have been wronged or insulted or slighted or ill-treated? Is this a wise expenditure of our personal abilities or would it be more effective to expend the same thought and effort in creating and liberating the power of love and good will in such practical ways as to change the attitude of our enemies toward us? Once again we must beware of confusing bluster with power.

## V. Is the Ideal Practicable?

Even though Jesus' ideal citizen of the New Order is seen to be a strong and positive personality, do we have anything more than a picture? Is this ideal at all possible of realization?

Turn to the Acts of the Apostles and read there how the powerful life began to show itself in the tradesmen and fishermen who had been with Jesus. After the crucifixion and the resurrection they come to the risen Lord with a question on their lips: "Master, is this the time at which you are about to restore the kingdom for Israel?" (Acts 1:6, Weymouth.)  They did not understand even then that Jesus was not concerned with an outward political kingdom.  But with the same patience which had characterized his dealings with them through the weeks and months just past, the Master made answer, "It is not for you to know about these things, but if it is power you want, you shall receive power" (Acts 1:7).

That promise of power came true.  The drama of the New Testament is the proof.  The powerful life was actually lived by these common men.  Not that mediocre intellects became brilliant or that obscure men were advanced to places of worldly power, but they knew in their own lives the mastery over evil.  They did not become suddenly perfect, nor were they lifted miraculously out of the realm where men battle with temptation, but the grip of lust was loosed and the power of the clean life was theirs.  The fear of death was no longer a specter and the power of the endless life was theirs.  The impulse to service sent them forth to tell the story of Jesus to the ends of the earth, and the power of the unselfish life was theirs.

These simple men found themselves living with God as a Father of infinite love and tenderness and with their fellow-men as brothers.  They were confident that the eternal Father was in control of human history and that He could be trusted with their lives.  Unique, manifold power was theirs, because they had left their nets and their desks and their places of business to heed the call, "*Follow me.*"

# CHAPTER VII

## THE INNER ATTITUDE

### SUGGESTIONS FOR PERSONAL STUDY

**Biblical Material.**

The importance of the inner attitude:

1. In relation to people. Mt. 5:21-26; 27-32; 7:1-5; 18:21-35.
2. In relation to "things." Mt. 6:19-34.
3. In relation to God. Mt. 6:1. Mt. 6:2, 3 cf. Mk. 14:3-9; 12:41-44. Mt. 6:5-15 cf. Luke 18:9-14. Mt. 6:16-18.
4. The inner attitude of the ideal citizen. Mt. 6:33.

**Preliminary Questions.**

These two chapters of the Sermon on the Mount (Mt. 5 and 6) are best studied as revealing the inner attitudes of the citizen of the New Order. Jesus is setting forth the way in which he will "feel" inside as he meets various people and relates himself to "things" and to God. Read all the references listed above with this in mind.

### I. The Citizen's Attitude Toward Other People.

1. What do you think Jesus means to say in Mt. 5:21-26? Is He referring to outward acts or inner attitudes?

2. Is it possible to do justice to a person in a single phrase or nickname? What are the dangers of branding a person

by a single cutting phrase? Is contempt a besetting sin of youth? Do you personally have to fight it?

3. What do you think of the practice of calling foreigners by contemptuous nicknames such as Chinks, Dagoes, Wops? May this have international consequences?

4. Read Jesus' searching words about reverence for the person of another. Mt. 5:27ff.

5. List the practical suggestions Jesus gives in regard to strained relations between individuals. Mt. 7:1-5, 18:21-35. Are any of these suggestions applicable to international rela tionships?

## II. The Citizen's Attitude Toward Things.

1. Read Mt. 6:19-34 and then attempt a paraphrase in your own words.

2. What is Jesus' definition of simplicity in this passage? Is He speaking here about inner attitudes or an outer program? What does it mean not to be anxious about clothes and food? What place do you think clothes and food have in life? Just why do you value them?

## III. The Citizen's Attitude Toward God.

1. Read Mt. 6:1-18 and translate it into the corresponding acts of worship which make up your religious observances.

2. Do the same temptations which Jesus describes assail you?

3. What is worship for? Does it mean to you real contact with God? If not, is the trouble with the form of worship or with your inner attitude?

4. Do you think there will be a new demand for reality in

acts of religion after the war? Is there such a demand now? Are you awake to this need?

## IV. The Inner Attitude of the Ideal Citizen.

Do you think Mt. 6:33 is an adequate statement of the citizen's inner attitude? Put it in your own words. Does it mean something positive and powerful to you?


It is a common delusion to suppose that we become something by copying its characteristic manifestations. In the old Greek comedy, "The Frogs," by Aristophanes, this delusion is amusingly illustrated. The principal character is a certain Dionysus, a luxury-loving, effeminate Greek. The play gets its plot from a dispute as to the respective merits of the two poets Æschylus and Euripides, both deceased. To settle the dispute Dionysus essays a visit to the lower regions in order to test the merits of the two poets by weighing their verses in a scale. The trip involves certain dangers, but Dionysus bethinks himself of a scheme. He will disguise himself as the mighty *H*eracles, so over his saffron gown he throws a lion's skin, and, seizing a huge club, he fares forth. But although he has the outer trappings of the valiant *H*eracles it is the trembling soul of the effeminate Dionysus beneath the lion's skin which is revealed through out the journey.

One does not become something simply by copying its characteristic manifestations, any more than Dionysus became *H*eracles by attempting to hide his saffron gown and dainty slippers with a lion's skin and a mighty club. *It is the inner attitude that counts.*

One does not become an orator by imitating the powerful voice of some favorite speaker, or a football player by donning the latest thing in moleskins, or a cultured man by lining his shelves with well-bound volumes or even by exposing himself to lectures. *H*e must have the "burning in his bones" if he would speak so that men will listen; he must play, as Theodore Roosevelt once said, "as though he carried an extra neck in his pocket," if he would win honors in any game; he must "have that thirst for knowledge which will compel the earth and the heavens, the past and the present to yield their lore, if he would become truly cultured. *It is the inner attitude that counts.*

Jesus put the emphasis here in the Sermon on the Mount. The Sermon on the Mount is not so much a program of conduct as it is an examination of *the motives* and *the spirit* which lie behind the things which the citizen of the New Order undertakes to do. Jesus is not outlining a new law which He proposes to substitute for the Jewish law or for any other system of conduct, but He is tracing right and wrong to their beginnings in "the secret laboratory of the spirit." These familiar words are like coins, long in circulation; they have been worn smooth by much handling. If we can restore the mint marks their priceless worth will again appear.

In the fifth and sixth chapters of Matthew Jesus sets forth the inner attitude of the Citizen of the New Order toward other *people,* toward *things* and toward *God.*

# THE INNER ATTITUDE

## I. The Citizen's Attitude Toward Other People.

A boy in a famous preparatory school, when asked on his first day to write out why he had come, wrote, "I came to learn how to get along with other people." In less than a dozen words he formulated the biggest problem in our world. To-day in blood and tears men are seeking its solution. Had Jesus anything to say concerning this problem?

You have heard that it was said by the men of old, Thou shalt not kill, and whoever kills shall be liable to the local court. But I tell you,

Every one who is angry with his brother shall be liable to the local court;

And whoever says to his brother, Ignoramus, shall be liable to the Sanhedrin.

And whoever says to his brother, *Fool*, shall be liable to the Gehenna of Fire. (Mt. 5:21-22, Kent.)

What does Jesus mean by these strange words? Does He really mean to say that if one calls another stupid or fool he will be liable to the supreme court of the land or to God's own judgment throne. Or is He talking about the *inner attitude of easy contempt and scorn* with which we view our fellows? This attitude seemed to Him a grave peril. Unless we dig out the roots of contempt and scorn from our lives they poison our whole thought about other people. How easy it is to get into the habit of summing up the characteristics of a person or a race in one facile, unjust, stinging phrase. Will the citizen of the new World Order talk about "Dagoes" or "Wops" or "Chinks"? or will he purge himself of all such personal or racial superciliousness? We deplore the horrors

95

of a world war, but too often the roots of war are sprouting in our own hearts.

Jesus made it perfectly plain that religious observances will not make up for this inner attitude of hate or scorn (Mt. 5:23-26).

He taught that respect for the person of another should be so genuine and fine as to master even the wayward imaginations (Mt. 5:27-30). He Himself won degraded men and women to new lives by persistently seeing divine possibilities within them.

Jesus laid great emphasis upon the inner attitude of the citizen toward any one who has wronged him. He suggested that the first thing to do is to go to the individual in person and try to make things right. "Now if thy brother sin, go show him his fault between thee and him alone" (Mt. 18:15). He knew how resentment feeds on suspicion and waxes fat on secret broodings. Then He counseled an attitude of forgiveness which loses all track of the number of offenses (Mt. 18:21). Can any one really forgive an offender if he is saying, "This makes the third time or the sixth time I've forgiven him; one more offense and I'll have revenge"?

In order that this obligation to forgive indefinitely might be rightly comprehended, Jesus told the story of the servant who was forgiven a debt of twenty million dollars and then refused to forgive his fellow servant a debt of twenty dollars (Mt. 18:23-25). Or again, Jesus says it is like a man who has a beam in his own eye and wants to take a splinter out of his brother's eye (Mt. 7:3-5). We have great need to be charitable and forgiving if that is to be the basis of our relationship to God (Mt. 6:12, 14, 15).

We are then to beware of an inner attitude of contempt

and scorn, we are to reverence and respect the person of another, and to be quick to forgive a real or a fancied wrong.

Jesus had more to say about our relations to other people. His great positive teaching of the inner attitude of love stands at the center of all his words and deserves a special chapter for its treatment.

## II. The Citizen's Attitude Toward "Things."

Jesus dealt very specifically with the citizen's attitude toward concrete "things," such as money, food and clothing (Mt. 6:19-34). His words seem very simple and straightforward, yet the Christian Church has always found it difficult to understand and apply them.

Christians have felt that Jesus meant his followers to have an "unworldly attitude toward things." But the word "unworldly" needs careful definition. What is *worldliness?* We have been inclined to say it is putting too high a value upon the things of this world, and we have been warned against this temptation. But that is exactly wrong, according to these great words of Jesus. Worldliness is putting too low a value upon things. It is assigning them only a temporal value. The citizen of the New Order places an infinitely higher value upon money and food and clothes and things in general than does the citizen of any temporal order. For he views all "things" with an eye to their eternal value. That seems to be the sole point Jesus is making in the parable of the unrighteous steward, who shrewdly used his position in order to make friends (Luke 16:1-13, esp. v. 9). Worldliness is hampered in two directions. It has a limited horizon and so only knows how to "lay up treasure on earth where moth and rust consume, and where thieves break through and steal." And then it is hampered by anxiety as to food and raiment and things in general (cf. Mt. 6: v. 25, 27, 28, 31, 34). The citizen of the New Order, on the other hand, values all "things" as they contribute to the lasting rule of God on earth.

It has been said that the attitude of the citizen toward "things" may be described by the word *simplicity*. But again we need to think carefully about the meaning of simplicity. We are learning on a large scale these days to say after Socrates, "How many things there are I do not need!" Men who go to the trenches and folk who stay at home are dispensing with numerous "things" only to find themselves just as happy and healthy and fit as before, and usually more so. It seems a good time to think about Jesus' words concerning simplicity.

What constitutes the simple life? Can we decide by enumerating the number of things we should have? That way many difficulties lie in wait. Practically every one can say, I live more simply than such and such a person. And is it all a matter of the number of things we have? Compare a country four-corners store with a big city department store. The one occupies a dingy frame building at the cross roads; the other a skyscraper which covers a city block. The proprietor of the one is at once manager, floor-walker, clerk, cashier, bookkeeper, parcel girl, delivery boy, and scrub woman; the other has its thousands of employees, each doing a specialized piece of work. The one has a single department; the other hundreds of departments. In the country store there is leisure and calm, in the city store bustle and rush and roar. Yet which way lies simplicity? Your business man will answer, in the direction of the city store, for the business synonym for simplicity is system.

Or think of the finely trained symphony orchestra with its hundred musicians playing strings and wood-winds and brasses and drums, attempting intricate scores of music. Compare with the symphony orchestra the town brass band composed of the dozen or so musically ambitious men who meet Saturday nights in the village band stand. Does simplicity lie in the direction of the town band? No, for simplicity in music means harmony. Contrast a German army corps with ten boys in a street fight. The German army corps is far simpler, because each boy is a field marshal, and discipline is simplicity in warfare.

Think of the most active man or woman you know, prominent in business, in society, in philanthropy, in religion, in politics, in æsthetics, and withal a lover of home. Now contrast the person of the narrowest interests. Is the latter necessarily an example of simplicity and the former of complexity of life? *Or is it the inner attitude that counts?*

What was Jesus' attitude? *H*e lived in the full round of the world's activities. He was a toiler, a teacher, a welcome guest at festivities, a man whom the common people heard gladly. He was no recluse. He seems not to have unnecessarily stripped himself of the things that make life enjoyable. There is almost a plaintive note in his declaration that the birds have nests and the foxes holes, but the Son of man does not have a place to lay his head. He shared the comfortable home of Lazarus and Mary and Martha with a genuine delight. Never once did He state a general rule as to the number of things a person must have in order to be a member of the Kingdom. The Rich Young Ruler had too

99

many possessions, but it seems to have been his inner attitude toward them that hampered him (Mt. 19:22).

Jesus traced simplicity to the attitude of the soul. It is conflicting desires that cause complexity of life. It doesn't matter in the least how complex the life in which we are called to live if our own inner attitude is clear and consistent. In this great passage (Mt. 6:19-34) Jesus sets forth four rules for simplicity of soul: first, a single set of values and that the highest (v. 19-21); second, a singleness of vision (v. 22, 23); third, a single master (v. 24); fourth, a single anxiety (v. 25-34 esp. v. 33).

## III. The Citizen's Attitude Toward God. Mt. 6:1-18.

There were three conventional forms of worship current in Jesus' day; *almsgiving, prayer,* and *fasting.* He did not condemn any one of these forms. He simply traced each act of worship to its underlying motive and judged it by its fruits. The object of worship is to bring the worshiper into living touch with God. Jesus seems to ask, "Do your acts of worship accomplish that end? Or is that the real object you have in view?" The Pharisees' goal, "to be seen of men," was easy of attainment, and when they had accomplished that object they were "paid in full." They could expect nothing more.

Almsgiving (Mt. 6:2-4) was the only outlet for general philanthropy in Jesus' day. What He said about almsgiving applies, then, to all the varied opportunities for relief and service which our needy world offers. Do we think of our giving as an act of worship? What is the inner motive that prompts us? Few are tempted to repeat the brass band giving of the hypocrites (Mt. 6:2) in literalistic fashion, but how complex our motives often are! Jesus was remarkably quick to sense the relation of the giver to the gift. He knew when it came from a genuine fellowship with God (Mk. 12:41-44; 14:6-9), and his appreciation of that sort of giving was warm and glad.

The gospels show that Jesus prayed more than He talked about prayer. It was the evident contrast between his prayer life and the display of religiosity which passed for prayer in synagogues and on street corners (Mt. 6:5) which challenged his disciples (Luke 11:1). And He pointed out the difference. It was a difference in inner attitude. First of all, in the case of the hypocrites, prayer was a matter of self-consciousness, and self-consciousness is always weakness. But for Jesus, prayer was a forgetting of self and a consciousness of God, "Our Father who art in heaven." It is by looking away from ourselves and beholding God that we are changed from the old self.

Then, prayer for the hypocrites was a kind of service they rendered God, and repetitions increased the merit (Mt. 6:7). That, said Jesus, is nothing but paganism (Mt. 6:7), and He made clear in the classic parable of the Pharisee and the Publican what real prayer means (Luke 18:9-14). The Pharisee simply congratulated God upon the excellencies of his workmanship in his particular case.

"But the tax-gatherer, standing far back, would not so much as lift his eyes to Heaven, but kept beating his breast and saying, O God, be reconciled to me, sinner that I am" (Weymouth).

Prayer, Jesus said, was to be brief and direct (Mt. 6:7, 8), persistent (Luke 11:5-8, 18:1-8), founded upon faith (Luke

17:5, 6, Mk. 11:22-24), and prefaced with a right relationship with fellowmen (Mk. 11:25).

The model prayer He gave his disciples (Mt. 6:9-13) was also surcharged with social sympathy. The individual is bound by each petition to his fellows. It is *our* Father to whom we pray, his Kingdom of men living as brothers for which we pray, and we may not ask for *my* but only for *our* daily bread. There is need for individual forgiveness, but the basis is "as we also have forgiven our debtors."

Jesus' words about fasting (Mt. 6:16-18) seem to have least to do with our modern life. Yet if we apply them to all forms of self-discipline they still convey a living message. One of the subtlest of temptations is to discipline oneself for some good end and then brag of the performance. Obviously that has nothing to do with worship of God. Only those forms of self-discipline, and that attitude toward them, which lead to real, vital, and constant touch with the Father are commended by Jesus.

"Beware of doing your good actions in the sight of men, in order to attract their gaze; if you do, there is no reward for you with your Father who is in Heaven" (Mt. 6:1, Weymouth). All acts of worship, however involved or simple, are liable to the same criticism. *It is the inner attitude that counts.*

## IV. The Inner Attitude of the Ideal Citizen. Mt. 6:33.

"Seek ye first his Kingdom and his righteousness." These words summarize the inner attitude of the citizen toward other people, toward "things" and toward God. All matters of form and ceremony are swept away by it. His inner attitude is to be a *search* which will call for the same wisdom and practical preparation and endurance which men devote to the quest of the North Pole, and the same zeal with which men dig for hidden treasure. This search will be the consuming passion of the citizen's life. It will be first for him. It will be a search for the things that are right from the top to the bottom of life. He will not rest until he lives in *right* relationship to other people and to "things" and to God. He will not rest until God's New Order is established on this earth.

The fires of war have burned away much that is cheap and superficial in our common life. Have we felt stirring within us the passion for a Kingdom that cannot be shaken and for realities which will endure?

The reconstruction of the world must begin by the reconstruction of our inner attitude toward people and "things" and God.

# CHAPTER VIII

## THE LAW OF LOVE

### SUGGESTIONS FOR PERSONAL STUDY

Biblical Material.

 1. Love as the first law. Luke 10:25-28; cf. Mk. 12:28-31; cf. Mt. 22:35-40.

 2. Misinterpretation.

  a. Simply applicable to a congenial neighbor. Luke 10:29-37; Mt. 5:43-47; cf. Luke 6:27, 32-35.

  b. Love to neighbors: sentiment? Mt. 23.

  c. Love to neighbors: charity? Mt. 6:2-4.

 3. Its real meaning.

  a. A matter of the heart and life. Mk. 12:32-34.

  b. A practical test. Mt. 7:12 cf. Luke 6:31.

It becomes very difficult to select from the gospels passages about love. Jesus did not define it any more than He defined the Kingdom of God. He was the embodiment of love and was in Himself the only satisfactory definition we know.

Only on a few occasions did He deal with the definition of love specifically, and then He accepted the Old Testament statement about it. He did, however, guard against certain misinterpretations of love, such as that it could. hardly be applied to those of another race or religion (Luke 10:25-37) or to enemies (Mt. 5:43-47) or that it was equivalent to occasional charity (Mt. 6:2-4). When we think about love we have to bear in mind, then, the whole course of his life.

## THE LAW OF LOVE

I. Review briefly the chapters on The Ideal Citizen and The Inner Attitude. Love is the key to all Jesus said about the character of the citizen of the New Order.

· II. Is there any danger to-day of misinterpreting the word *neighbor?* Are you tempted to limit it to people of like tastes, of like religion, of like race, of like nationality? Did Jesus limit it at all? Has the Christian any right to limit it?

III. Is love the same thing as sentiment? Read Mt. 23. Is it possible to love people for whom you feel no emotion of affection? Is love something you can will to do? *How* would you express a love which is without sentiment? When you do some act of genuine service for another does real affection sometimes result?

IV. How is it possible to reconcile personal ambition and love for one's neighbor? Does it depend upon the goal set before the individual? Is it possible to adopt life aims which will at the same time call for the highest personal development and genuine service for, and love of, one's neighbor?

V. What do you think of "brotherhood" as a modern synonym for love? Does it include the same ideas? Does it avoid the common misinterpretations of love? Is it subject to the same dangers as neighborliness?

VI. What do you think Christ's law of love means in terms of business life, international relations? Can a young man or woman start to-day to live a life upon that principle of love to neighbor and succeed?

A certain lawyer once asked Jesus this question, "What shall I do to inherit eternal life?" Jesus drew from him an answer to his own query: "Thou shalt love the Lord thy God with all thy heart, and with all thy soul and with all thy strength and with all thy mind; and thy neighbor as thyself" (Deut. 6:5; Lev. 19:18). "A right answer," said Jesus, "do that, and you shall live" (Luke 10:27-28).

"And thy neighbor as thyself." These words Jesus drew from the lawyer. The lawyer quoted them from the Old Testament. They are perfectly orthodox words and not in the least sensational. And yet we probably are agreed that love of neighbor is the central teaching of Jesus. The sensational thing about his law of love was that He actually put it into practice in his own life and summoned his disciples to a like endeavor. It has always been orthodox to believe in loving one's neighbor but it has always been startling when people have really tried to do it. And as a matter of fact it is the one part of Jesus' program which the world has never accepted, although they are ready to accept much of the doctrine and paraphernalia of institutional Christianity.

Since the world has been so slow about accepting Jesus' law of love, we are forced to ask, Is it reasonable? Will it work? Is it practicable in our kind of a world, people being as they are? Ought we really to try to love our neighbor as ourselves? These questions give rise to at least three others. Who is our neighbor? What is love? When is love to be applied to a neighbor? We need to clear away certain misinterpretations and misapplications of Jesus' thought here, for it has sometimes happened that many who are outwardly his followers have never understood his program of love to one's neighbor, while some have lived out that program even though alienated from his professed disciples.

# THE LAW OF LOVE

## I. Jesus' Program of Love is Bigger than Neighborliness.

What does it mean to love one's neighbor? The obvious answer is neighborliness, that genial good-natured relation with friends and acquaintances whose back yards are next our own. Love to neighbor means that, surely. If we cannot live on terms of positive good will and serviceableness with those with whom we have most frequent dealings, the law of love condemns us, and we must suffer the consequences of its inexorable working, in the bitterness and petty enmity of neighborhood quarrels. Perhaps it is as difficult to live out the law of love with one's neighbors as anywhere in all the world of human relationships.

But Jesus evidently meant something more sweeping than amicable dooryard diplomacy. The Pharisees had gone that far. Let them choose their neighbors and they could be neighborly. Even the lawyer was ready to love his neighbor if he was the right sort. If Jesus meant only that, then it might be possible to be genuinely Christian by a judicious selection of neighbors. But we congratulate ourselves upon our ability to see beyond such a narrow application of love. Jesus extended infinitely the limits of the word neighbor. No cliques or groups or class or social order or religious or political sect could claim Him while He walked the hills and dales of Palestine. He called every man in need his neighbor, and his disciples to-day will be no narrower.

## II. Love versus Sentiment.

A second misinterpretation of love of neighbor has to do with the meaning of love. There are people who understand full well what Jesus meant by neighbor, who think that love as Jesus used the word is the synonym of sentiment. To such people love of neighbor means an affectionate reaction to every one whom they chance to meet. If the sensation does not appear they think they have suffered a relapse in their Christianity.

But such a sentimental attitude toward the world is not what Jesus meant by love. He who undertakes to interpret love as such a sickly sentiment will meet with one of two results. If he undertakes it honestly he will give the whole thing up as an impossible, foolish and impracticable dream. People will take advantage of his innocence and he will decide that after all it's a cold, hard world and every man must look out for himself. On the other hand, if he does not undertake this program of love in dead earnest he will soon be continually simulating an affection he does not actually feel.

If ever any one loved his neighbor genuinely, Jesus did. But He did not react sentimentally to every one He chanced to meet. Read again the terrible woes recorded in Matthew 23: "Alas for you, Scribes and Pharisees, hypocrites, . . . you blind guides, straining out the gnat while you gulp down the camel. Alas for you, Scribes and Pharisees, hypocrites, for you wash clean the outside of the cup or dish, while within they are full of greed and self-indulgence. Alas for you, Scribes and Pharisees, hypocrites, for you are just like white-washed sepulchers, full of dead men's bones. O serpents, O vipers' brood, how are you to escape condemnation to Gehenna?" (Weymouth.)

It is not that the world does not need more human kindness and tenderness and sympathy—is there anything our world needs so much? But the love of Christ finds its source much deeper than any mere surface sentiment. The love Jesus exemplified was a moral quality, subject to the will, not to the caprice of moods and emotions. It was something that functioned even toward disagreeable and unpleasant people, and one cannot love a disagreeable individual or a disagreeable nation unless love has claimed more than his fickle emotions. It must have captured his intellect and his will. As followers of Jesus Christ, as those who draw inspiration from the lives of the disciples, we are challenged to redeem the word love from its flabby associations.

### III. The Law of Love Not Emergency Legislation.

Most of us have seen deeper than either of these surface interpretations of love to neighbor. We do not think Jesus meant by neighbor only those whose back yards touch our own. Nor do we think that love is equivalent to sentiment. But we have been guilty of thinking of the great law of love as a sort of emergency legislation rather than as the law of life. Have we missed the point of the parable of the Good Samaritan? The parable of the Good Samaritan is a vivid, telling picture drawn from life. Jesus tells the story in answer to the lawyer's question, "But what is meant by my neighbor?" He replies:

A man was once on his way down from Jerusalem to Jericho when he fell among robbers, who after both stripping and beating him went away, leaving him half dead. Now a priest happened to be going down that way, and on seeing him, passed by on the other side. In like manner a Levite also came to the place, and seeing him, passed by on the other side. But a certain Samaritan, being on a journey, came where he lay, and seeing him, was moved with pity. He went to him, dressed his wounds with oil and wine, and bound them up. Then placing him on his own mule, he brought him to an inn, where he bestowed every care on him. The next day he took out two shillings and gave them to the innkeeper.

Take care of him, he said, and whatever further expense you are put to, I will repay you on my next visit.

Which of those three seems to have acted like a fellow man to him who fell among the robbers?

The one who showed pity, he replied.

Go, said Jesus, and act in the same way. (Luke 10:30-37, Weymouth.)

Of course the point of this classic story is that the Samaritan's friendly, loving act was directed toward a member of a hostile race, while a priest and a Levite, fellow countrymen and co-religionists of the poor man, had already "passed by on the other side of the road." The lawyer's question, "Who is my neighbor?" was answered in full. If a despised Samaritan stepping across the racial line to help a Jew in distress, especially after that Jew had been abandoned to his fate by proud representatives of his own religion, is to be thought of as a concrete definition of brotherly love, doubtless the lawyer needed to revise his definition of neighbor. Now the lawyer had been forced to admit that the Samaritan was the real neighbor in this case, so there was no chance for him to squirm out of his tight situation.

But we have looked at this parable too often as though the lawyer's question were, "How shall I love my neighbor?" And then we have taken Jesus' answer as a full and final definition of love: "Pick up the wounded and beaten man along the track of life, bathe his wounds, take care of him." That is to say, love finds its place of action by the roadside of life. It is an occasional thing. It is not to be thought of as the main business of life, but rather something to be expressed outside of business hours or incidentally. There are, to be sure, plenty of robbed and beaten men who need to be picked up and cared for, and love of neighbor will always find abundant opportunity for expression in the work of rescue. But the law of love is more than emergency legislation. It is meant to apply to all life.

As we think about our world to-day, does it not seem as though Jesus' teaching of love to neighbor had been accepted only as emergency legislation? On the battlefields of Europe men are being "beaten and left for dead." The Red Cross Samaritan does not pass by on the other side, but comes to the injured man, picks him up, bathes his wounds, pouring on oil and wine more scientifically and successfully than the original Samaritan knew how to do. It is a beautiful and effective expression of the love which Jesus taught. But Christian nations are still shooting the men down and will continue to do so until the end of time unless we learn that Jesus meant love to be something more than emergency legislation.

## IV. Love as the Law of Life.

The love Christ taught is neither narrow, superficial nor occasional. He set forth love as the law of life. It is indeed the *whole law* of life. Upon one occasion the Pharisees asked him as a test question, "Teacher, which is the greatest commandment in the Law?" He replied in the words of the Old Testament, "Love God with your entire personality and your neighbor as yourself" The whole of the Law and the Prophets is summed up in these two commandments (Mt. 22:34-40). According to Mark's record (12:28-34) one of the scribes commended this answer and Jesus turned to him and said, "You are not far from the Kingdom of God."

The other New Testament writers understood the fundamental character of Jesus' teaching at this point. Paul in his letter to the Roman Christians tells them that "*He* who loves his neighbor has fulfilled the law" (Romans 13:8-10). And in a letter to the Galatian Christians he writes, "The whole law is fulfilled in one word, even in this, Thou shalt love thy neighbor as thyself" (Galatians 5:14). And James writes, "If you fulfill the royal law according to the scriptures, thou shalt love thy neighbor as thyself, you do well" (James 2:8). Neither of these writers treats love as a matter of impulse and emotion, but as a matter of will. It is commanded of the Christians. They look upon it as a reasonable commandment. Love is that principle under the power and guidance of which we are to live our lives. This love to neighbor is an inner attitude which will find expression in forgiveness (Mt. 18:15, 21, 22), in a unique way of dealing with aggressors (Mt. 5:38-48), in charitable judgments of others (Mt. 7:1-5), and in reverence and respect for the person of another (Mt. 5:21-28).

Jesus did not give any formal definition of love. It was not his custom to give formal definitions. He showed what love is in essence and practice by a series of dramatic illustrations, such as the story of the Good Samaritan (Luke 10:25-37). In the Golden Rule He made unmistakable the practical meaning of love: "Act toward your fellow-men exactly as you would have them act toward you" (Luke 6:31, Mt. 7:12). He was Himself the living embodiment of this great law of life, and we understand love best as we understand Him.  He lived out his program of neighborly love on the plains of common human experience.

. People have said that Jesus' teaching is too high and hard, that it could be worked out only in a world of saints.  But when we read the Sermon on the Mount we find that although it is high indeed, in every single case the principles of Jesus are set over against the conditions, circumstances and personalities of our world.  Conduct is outlined toward a brother who is provoking, enemies who are insulting.  Jesus seems to have in mind just the suspicious, unjust, hostile, self-seeking communities with which we have to deal and of which we form a part.  This entire program of living is keyed to the present struggle with evil, and Jesus evidently meant it for folk like us.

How is it possible to live this life of love to-day?  How, in a practical way, are we to give expression to it?  If Jesus did not mean by love anything narrow or emotional or occasional, and if He did mean that positive inner attitude which was the power behind his own life, what does love mean in our world?  The word *brotherhood* best expresses, perhaps, this principle of Jesus in our own vocabulary.

It is a splendid word, this word brotherhood.  It takes us back to the nursery.  What did it mean to be a brother or a sister in childhood days?  As people look back through the mists of the years they are tempted to grow sentimental about the delights of those early days.  But when we think calmly and without emotion we will remember that the nursery was no such idealistic dream of peace and joy as sentimentalists would have us think.  There was tempest as well as sunshine. It was a little world in itself, with most of the tragedies as well as the comedies represented.

But the law of the rightly ordered nursery, the law of brotherhood which makes it a fit symbol of Jesus' love to neighbor, was the *law of sharing up*. If there was one apple and six children the apple must go into six pieces. Sometimes there were howls and protestations, and who would maintain that he felt any great glow of joy over the just division of the fruit! Were there sometimes little brothers or even little sisters who would have preferred the whole apple? But because they were brothers and sisters it had to be divided. That was the law of brotherhood. And is there any more profound definition of brotherhood than this: *It is the will to include as many as possible in my own success and joy and happiness. It is the will to spend my powers in the service of our common humanity.* How many brothers do we have? With how many people do we *will* to share the good things of life?

Jesus' declaration, "Love your neighbor," was nothing less than a reasonable life program. He meant that young men and women should choose their life work with sole reference to the expression of the brotherhood in their hearts. The work to which the citizen dedicates his energies is to be that line of endeavor in which his personal powers can be most serviceable to humanity. We have thought of Christ's law of love as a counsel of despair or of martyrdom. Jesus thought of it as the motive governing every practical decision in life, material as well as spiritual. It was so in his own life. He faced and fought and put behind Him the temptation to use his superb powers for personal ends. From beginning to end He shunned every temptation to the sensational and responded eagerly to every genuine human need. Very early in his ministry an officer of the King's court came to Him to heal his dying son. "Unless you and others see miracles and marvels," said Jesus, "nothing will induce you to believe." "Sir," pleaded the officer, "come down before my child dies." And Jesus responded instantly (John 4:46-50). Human need called forth all the great powers of Jesus. No one ever lived who was so successful in helping other people. He helped people who had tried discipline and failed, who had tried to live by a good program and failed. Where precept failed, love succeeded. Jesus loved men into the Kingdom. And one writer, pondering on his life, cried out in a burst of eloquence: How *God* must love the world to have sent one like Jesus into it! (John 3:16.)

It has been said that two types of men stand contrasted in our world, the scientist and the politician, the one, the most conspicuous success, the other the most conspicuous failure. The labors of the scientist have added more to the welfare of mankind than the efforts of any other. The labors of the politician have resulted in war. But in so far as the scientist has succeeded he has exemplified Christ's law of love. Perhaps from an emotional standpoint he has made little pretense of love to neighbor. But his motive has been a selfless exertion of will and intellect in the service of truth, and consequently in the service of fellow-men. This is one phase, at least, of Christ's law of love.

The New Order that is to be will have *love* as its throbbing heart, pumping the warm, life-giving blood to every part of the whole human body.

# CHAPTER IX

## THE CITIZEN AND SOCIETY

### SUGGESTIONS FOR PERSONAL STUDY.

**Biblical Material.**

1. The social platform of Jesus. Luke 4:16-22.
2. The social test of the Messiah. Luke 7:18-23.
3. The social interpretation of the Beatitudes. Luke 6:20-26.
4. The Lord's Prayer socially considered. Mt. 6:9-13.

Here, as in our study of the law of love, we have, scripturally speaking, an embarrassment of riches. Every requirement or characteristic of the citizen which we have studied so far is to fit him for life in a new society or Kingdom of God. Can you think of a single characteristic of the citizen studied so far which is not meant specifically to create a *better social order?* The Beatitudes (Mt. 5:1-12) seemed like a description of a hermit saint, but we found them to be capable of a most vigorous social interpretation. Luke, indeed, has a version of the Beatitudes entirely keyed to a social readjustment, by which the poor and the needy will be cared for.

I. Read Luke 4:16-22. Paraphrase the passage which Jesus quoted from Isaiah, substituting modern social conditions which Jesus would have included in his program of work. Would He have included under "good tidings to the poor" and "release to captives" people who work in sweat shops, children who work in glass factories and cotton mills, breaker boys who spend long hours bending over coal chutes, telegraph boys sent with their messages into the underworld of vice?

II. What does it mean to "follow Jesus" in the working out of a program like that outlined by Him at Nazareth? What are our obligations toward the physically and indus trially hampered in our own community?

III. Read Luke 7:18-23. John's perplexity concerning Jesus was probably due to the fact that he did not see the big results he had expected from the Messiah. Jesus had spent most of his time working with individuals and had not changed things much as yet. Do you think Jesus ex pected individuals whom He helped to help others? Was that his plan of making a new society or order in the world? Has it succeeded or failed? In so far as it has failed, what is the cause for the failure? What causes doubt about Christianity to-day? Is it because Christianity has not yet created the New Order of society which Jesus outlined? Is this in some measure due to the fact that Christians think of their religion as a "good thing" for themselves? Does being a Christian mean to you primarily getting spiritual satisfaction for yourself or getting in shape to bring in a better order of society? Look at that last question again.

IV. Read Mt. 6:9-13. Is there anything in that prayer which refers to the individual apart from his fellows or is it all a "social" prayer? Think about your own prayer life. Do you ever pray for any one besides yourself and your own relatives? Have you caught the spirit of Jesus?

# THE WAY OF CHRIST

In the midst of Jesus' active ministry He faced one day a crowd of more than five thousand people. They were in an uninhabited place, for the crowd had followed Jesus even when He sought seclusion. Matthew tells us that "He felt compassion for them and cured those of them who were out of health" (Mt. 14:14, Weymouth). As He thus ministered to them the afternoon wore away, and the time for the evening meal drew near. The disciples were troubled about the situation and they came to Him with this anxious query, "This is an uninhabited place and the best of the day is now gone; shall we send the people away to go into the villages and buy something to eat?"

We can imagine that they were thinking, "This is too big a problem for us. See what a vast multitude is present. If there were only a few we might share our supplies, but how can we handle this crowd?" And perhaps they were even saying, "The Master is concerned with the souls of these people, their religious welfare, and He cannot be expected to deal with a food famine." But Jesus' reply was, "They need not go away; you yourselves must give them something to eat." The story goes on to relate how Jesus organized that crowd, made use of the meager supplies on hand, five biscuits and two sardines, and through the power of God and the cooperation of the disciples the needs of the multitude were more than met (Mt. 14:13-21).

To-day the disciples of Jesus have upon their lips this same question, "Master, what shall we do with the multitudes? How shall we meet their needs, physical as well as spiritual? It is too big a problem for us. See, they are hungry, and ill-clad and overworked and underfed and poorly housed, and not properly educated, and we don't see where these things are to come from. Shall we send them away to shift for themselves? Perhaps, as your disciples, these things are not a part of our business anyhow. Perhaps we are only to try to save their souls and not be concerned about their bodies. But the living Christ is saying to-day, "They need not go away; you yourselves must give them something to eat." ·

It seems a long journey from the five thousand men, who thronged the shores of little Galilee almost nineteen centuries ago, to the teeming millions of our great cities; from their simple life to the complicated tangle of modern industrial and social conditions. But once again the disciples of Jesus are thinking about the multitudes in their common needs. They are facing the social life of to-day and saying, Master, what shall we do with this crowd?

Good News for the common life of men, or the social gospel—this is the compelling need of our world. It is a gospel which begins with the individual and is "good news" for him, but which widens with his widening life and is equally good news for the family and business life and the nation and the world, a gospel which is good news for despised races and for little children who have to work in factories and for the poor and the weak-minded and the physically inefficient, and for womanhood the world over, and for the multimillionaire who often needs good news as much as any one, and for all the needs of our common humanity.

The person who has not felt this need must have been living a hermit's life. In the Middle Ages young men and women of the best type were mightily attracted by the monastic ideal, just because that seemed the only way of living the truly Christian life in the midst of an evil world. The world is evil enough to-day but the challenge lies in just the opposite direction. It is a challenge to put the yeast of Christlike character in contact with the mass of humankind, with the confident expectation that if the yeast be genuine it will sooner or later leaven the whole mass.

## I. The Need for a Social Gospel.

That the good news of Jesus needs to be applied to society as well as to the individual is not a new discovery, but it has been given new emphasis in our time. Perhaps we have felt this need because of our inquisitive spirit.

Suppose a man gets drunk; he is personally disgraced, his home is imperiled and impoverished and he is rendered inefficient for his work. Is it simply enough to say that that man is a sinner? Our inquisitiveness leads us to ask why he got drunk. Was it simply because he was a bad man through and through or a thoughtless man, or were there contributing causes which were partly to blame? We inquire into his life and discover that he lives in a tenement under conditions that seem to us extraordinarily dull and uninviting, not to say repulsive. We ask about his work and find that he operates a machine which performs a single minute process in the making of a pair of shoes. We can scarcely endure the monotony of watching the machine for ten minutes, but he must watch it for weeks and months and years. The more machine-like his motions, the more efficient he is. There is little chance for pride in his work.

We ask about his pleasures and discover that he has no automobile and consequently has to depend for his thrills on whatever is to be had. He has no club save the corner saloon, and there concentrated thrills are provided at five cents the glass, and he seeks to forget his troubles in the ways society has provided just as we forget our troubles in the socially recognized pleasures of our group. And we are led to ask, Is not society the sinner as well as this man? It is possible to live the Christian life under conditions like that, for men and women have done it, and are doing it to-day, but would it not be vastly easier if the conditions of life were more favorable?

Or here is a man at the other end of the social scale who has gathered together a hundred millions of dollars. His methods of acquiring it have been corrupt and unjust. We say he is a malefactor of great wealth. He has no business with so much money. Too much power is gathered in the hands of one man and even if he use the power wisely and well it is wrong that he should have it. But his reply is, "I am not to blame. Society is the sinner. It is the way society is organized that has enabled me to gain this great wealth. I am but a cog, even if a big cog, in a vast machine. These corrupt practices which have made me rich are the common ways of the world. The men who cry me down have tried the same corrupt means, only less successfully. Society lays its richest rewards at my feet and praises me for what I have done." Is there something to be said for the argument of this rich man?

Or here is a college student. For four years he lives apart from the common burdens and responsibilities of life. He develops habits of idleness, selfishness, and extravagance. He forgets that he is living upon the fruits which others have grown, that these days set apart are always bought with the life blood and the tears of somebody. *H*as he the same excuse? Society makes possible, even encourages, such a life in college days. It counts upon the sowing of wild oats, laughs at questionable exploits, expects little hard work, tolerates a code of morals which could not prevail else where.

And so through all the levels of society each man has the same plausible excuse for his shortcomings and his sins, until we cry out to God for a gospel that shall meet these conditions. It is not enough to pick up the men who lie wounded and bleeding by the way that leads from Jerusalem to Jericho; we want to deal with the bands of robbers that infest that district. It is good to pluck firebrands from the burning, but what is to be done about putting out the fires that waste and destroy? The challenge of the times is for a social gospel to reinforce and make effectual the individual gospel. We want a good news for the world. *H*ad Jesus such a gospel to offer?

## II. Jesus' Social Ideal.

Jesus began his work by saying, "The time has fully come and the Kingdom of God is close at hand: repent and believe this Good News." He had nothing to say about individuals apart from this social ideal of a kingdom or rule of God. His picture of society was that of a family—a world-wide, peaceable, serviceable brotherhood. In studying about his idea of this New Order we saw how it partakes of the very spirit of democracy. The Jews had always thought of the better day which was to come in social rather than in individual terms. It was not to be a better day for a few or even many individuals but a better day for the nation as a whole.

Jesus *widened* this ideal by denying the national limitations. It was for Gentiles as well as Jews. He *deepened* it by making it a spiritual rather than a mere political kingdom. He *purified* it by revealing God as Father and men as his sons and, therefore, as brothers. He *made it a present possibility* rather than a dream for the future by showing how this New Order of affairs may begin now in the hearts of men, and that however small and insignificant its beginnings, we may confidently expect that it will grow. He *made it a present reality* in his own life and in his relations with others. He set forth the only motive which has ever proved effectual in social endeavor, a love as spontaneously alive to a neighbor's need as to its own. Jesus gave the world a social gospel, the Good News of the Kingdom of God, in which Kingdom the king is a divine Father and all the subjects are sons and all the sons are brothers.

When Jesus came to his home city, Nazareth, He seemed to feel the necessity of explaining to his own townspeople the nature of the mission He had undertaken in the world. He entered into the synagogue and read this wonderful passage from the prophecy of Isaiah:

The spirit of the Lord is upon me,
Because he has anointed me to proclaim Good News to the poor;
He has sent me to pronounce release to the prisoners of war
And recovery of sight to the blind:
To send away free those whom tyranny has crushed,

# THE WAY OF CHRIST

To proclaim the year of acceptance with the Lord.
(Isaiah 61 :1, 2.)

` Then He proceeded to say to them, "To-day is this scripture fulfilled in your hearing." His active sympathy with those who were the victims of the social order of his own time, his shocking fellowship with publicans and sinners, his words of cheer for the poor and of warning for the rich, the democratic spirit which He describes as the spirit of the New Order, his work of ministry to the sick of body as well as to the sick of heart, his entire life and teaching, is a commentary upon that inaugural at Nazareth.

And yet, in spite of the superb sympathy and service which Jesus rendered to the downtrodden classes and races and in spite of his fair and just social ideal, there are those who find his social attitude disappointing. If He so sympathized with the unfortunate victims of the social order of his day, why did He not advocate tearing up the old social order and substituting something better? Instead of that He actually spent his time helping individuals. He lavished Himself upon individuals. "He had always leisure to attend to the humblest; even the children could claim his time."

John the Baptist seemed to feel this difficulty. He did not see things happening in the sweeping way he had expected. He had thought the Messiah would inaugurate tremendous changes. And so he sent from his prison cell, asking, "Are you the Coming One or is there a different person that we are to expect?" (Mt. 11:3.) Jesus' answer was almost a repetition of his inaugural at Nazareth: "Go and report to John what you see and hear; blind eyes receive sight and cripples walk; lepers are cleansed and deaf ears hear; the dead are raised to life and the poor have the Good News proclaimed to them." He seems to have committed Himself to personal service with the social ideal in view.

It is true that Jesus did not say anything about socialism or trade unionism or political revolution or economic theories or even the equivalents of those things in his own day. He was dealing with a people who were very eager for political and social revolution. They were tinder ready for any spark to set them in flame. From the Temptation to the Cross Jesus resolutely set his face against committing the New Order to such agencies. He knew that no mere redistribution of property or social reorganization would bring in the New Order if the people who made up the readjusted social order had the same kind of hearts as before. The New Order is first of all an inner spirit which seeks to find outer forms of expression. This was the reason why Jesus sought to create a group of individuals who have this social ideal and are committed unreservedly to it *from the inside out.*

### III. Jesus' Attitude Toward Social Institutions.

If we cannot find in the teachings of Jesus a specific social program, we do find an attitude of approach and the values to be conserved. Jesus, standing at the center of the same circles of social life which surround us, claimed them all for the New Order.

The first of these circles is the home. "Jesus throughout his public career was singularly homeless. The Son of Man had nowhere to lay his head." With the most touching solitariness of spirit He "stretched forth his hand toward his disciples and said, Behold, my mother and my brethren."

Yet the religion of this homeless teacher was, in its character and symbolism, a religion of the home. God was a father, man was his child, and the communion of man with God was the intimacy of child with parent. "The self-reproach of sin was nothing else than homesickness; and the first utterance of a repentant life was: 'I will arise and go to my father.'" *

We shall expect to find that Jesus guarded closely an institution which offered the fittest symbolism for the New Order. He encouraged marriage (Mt. 19:4, 5), and struck at everything that threatened the home (Mt. 19:6, Mk. 10:10-12). Nothing reveals his attitude toward the home more than his love of children. In the same chapter in which Mark records Jesus' sharp words about the dangers threatening the home, he records the beautiful tenderness of the childless Master for the children who were brought to Him (Mk. 10:13-15). "He took them in his arms and blessed them lovingly, one by one" (Weymouth). He had something to say about family life also. We are not to suppose that He meant that the Golden Rule was simply for extra-family observance. That inner attitude toward other people finds its first and most constant chance for expression in the home circle, and we are awkward and selfish neighbors because we are habitually that kind of sons and daughters. In regard to the relations between parents and children He taught that the duties of the latter to the former are real and in no sense formal (Mk. 7:6-13).

But with all his love for the home, Jesus taught that it

* Peabody, The Christian Life in the Modern World, pp. 44, 45.

was not to be an end in itself but simply the highway into the larger Kingdom of God. The family whose code is, "Me and my wife, my son John and his wife, us four and no more," defeats the New Order of Jesus almost as completely as do lax divorce laws and social immorality. Was this part of Jesus' meaning when He said, "If any one comes to me and hates not his father and mother and brothers and sisters, yes, and his own life also, he cannot be my disciple"? (Luke 14:26.) To Jesus the family meant, then, a stage in the realization of that universal family, the Kingdom of God.

The second of the social circles which Jesus dealt with was the business world. Jesus must have been decidedly attracted by business enterprises. He had spent the larger part of his life in the thick of them. He draws his illustrations from three principal fields—nature, the family, and the business world, and it is from the last that He draws most copiously when He is talking about the kind of character which the New Order will produce. He seems to have thought of the business life as a kind of school for character. His teachings are full of shepherds, merchants, fishermen, laborers, householders, builders; in fact, all the varied business enterprises of the day are reflected in the pages of the gospels. It was a very different sort of industrial and commercial life from our own, but we have only to substitute the inventor, the manufacturer, the wage-earner, the trustee, the contractor, for the business figures of the gospel, to see the same fundamental problems which appear to-day.

It would be foolish to seek to find detailed information about the complex problems of to-day, but we may be sure that

Jesus believed that one could be a citizen of the New Order and engage in these necessary occupations. Does it follow that when business is so conducted that the principles of the New Order are not observed Jesus would advocate a reorganization of business? He did set forth two fundamental principles which are being increasingly recognized. The first was the law of service: "Whoever would be chief among you must be your servant" (Mk. 10:43). The second was the law of humanization: "Is not a man of more value than a sheep?" Jesus asked (Mt. 12:12). In a day when business to many seems, nothing other than a form of piracy or warfare, these two principles of service and of humanization are steadily gaining ground.

Jesus had little to say about his own nation as a nation. The peculiar circumstances of the Jews made it difficult for Him to express the profound patriotism which underlies all his teaching without stirring a revolutionary spirit. Revolt against Rome would have been suicidal, and besides, Jesus was not willing to permit the ideal of the New Order to be identified with the passion, bitterness and narrow nationalism of the Jewish revolutionists. His nation was to Jesus the divinely appointed and prepared instrument for bringing in the New Order upon earth. He betrays not the least interest in mere political greatness as such. His thought is all keyed to the coming of the wider brotherhood of man upon earth.

Jesus did not despair of a single social institution. He claimed them all for the new Kingdom. No one ever saw more clearly their weaknesses and wrongs, but He seemed to trust implicitly that the reign of God in the hearts of individuals would eventually mean the rescuing of every worthy social institution for the New Order

## IV. The Social Attitude of the Citizen.

In one paragraph Paul has two paradoxical sayings which seem to gather up the whole attitude of the citizen toward society. He is writing to the Galatian churches and he tells them to "bear one another's burdens and thus fulfill the law of Christ." But he has scarcely finished that word of advice before he seems to contradict it by saying, "For each man must bear his own burden" (Gal. 6:1-6). It is not a real contradiction, however, but a great philosophy of life. The context shows that what Paul means is that although every man has to bear the burden of moral responsibility for himself and no one can assume that burden for him, at the same time Christ's law is that we shall help to bear the outward burdens of all the needy.

The citizen of the Kingdom will say in every situation, "My responsibility is to make my decision right, whatever the circumstances are, and also to make the circumstances right whatever other men's decisions are." This is the two fold responsibility of the citizen of the Kingdom toward society in all its forms. We cannot make decisions for other people nor are we responsible for their decisions save as we have failed to make every circumstance surrounding their lives helpful toward a right decision.

It is largely through social sympathy and service that the citizen of the New Order gets his spiritual growth. We do not become spiritually-minded by saying, Go to, now, I will become spiritually-minded. God looks after our spiritual growth; we are not compelled to bear that burden. Our burden is the social burden. As we live our lives at home, in the community, at school, at work, in the church, "bearing one another's burdens," God will take care of the inner life.

# CHAPTER X

## THE CAPITAL CITY OF THE KINGDOM

### SUGGESTIONS FOR PERSONAL STUDY

**Biblical Material.**

1. Living near the boundary lines.
    a. The professional line. Mk. 2:1-7.
    b. The line of prejudice. Mk. 2:13-16.
    c. The ceremonial line. Mk. 2:18.
    d. The traditional line. Mk. 2:23, 24; 3:1, 2.
    e. The geographical line. John 4:19, 20.
    f. The line of calculating goodness. Mt. 18:21.
    g. The moral line. Mk. 10:17-20.
2. Living at the capital of the Kingdom.
    a. The power of God instead of professionalism. Mk. 2:8-12.
    b. Sympathy instead of narrow prejudice. Mk. 2:17.
    c. Fresh vitality instead of ceremonialism. Mk. 2:19-22.
    d. Human needs above tradition. Mk. 2:25-28; 3:3-6.
    e. A worshipful spirit instead of prescribed places. John 4:21-24.
    f. Hearty (Mt. 18:35) instead of calculating forgiveness. Mt. 18:22, 35.

g. A sacrificial venture instead of easy morality. Mt. 10:21, 22.

I. Make a careful study of the boundary lines as laid out by the Pharisees. Is there any danger of living near such boundary lines to-day? What do you understand by "professionalism" in religion? Do you know people who have such a spirit in their religious life? Are you entirely free from it yourself? What fences of prejudice exist to-day? In the light of Mark 2:13-17, what should the Christian's attitude be toward such fences? Think of the people you are prejudiced against. Put down the reasons why you dislike them. Are these reasons Pharisaical or Christlike? Can you think of any tradition in your personal life or in the life of your school or community which is Pharisaical? How would Christ regard such a tradition?

II. Now ignore the particular boundary line disputes which the Pharisees brought to Jesus and think of their attitude as a whole. How would you describe it? Does the word legalistic correctly characterize it? Face this same question yourself. Does religion to you mean simply lists of things you ought or ought not to do? Does it mean anything more than boundary lines?

III. Contrast Jesus' attitude. Why was He indifferent to many boundaries the Pharisees thought important? Read again his answers to their criticisms. What was the outstanding difference between Jesus' own religious life and that of the Pharisees? Test your own life by the qualities which have appeared in our study of Jesus.

It has often proved perilous to live near boundary lines. The buffer state always suffers first and most severely in time of warfare. And yet men live on in the border country.

The peril of living on the border between hostile nations is simply an illustration of the peril of border living in general, for kingdoms of thought and conduct have their boundaries which are disputed as vigorously as are territorial limits. This has always been particularly true about the boundary lines between the Kingdoms of Right and Wrong. The border region of these two kingdoms is the most thickly populated district in the moral and spiritual life of humanity.

Very few people are willing to admit that they live in the Kingdom of Wrong. Even if it can be shown that they are actually dwelling there, they would probably insist that they are by no means permanent residents but simply temporary inhabitants of the district for business or social or political purposes. But as far back as the memory of mankind reaches there has been a bitter struggle on as to just where the division line fence between right and wrong, and good and evil, and truth and falsehood should be run.

## I. Boundary Lines.

This problem was absorbing the attention of the religious leaders of the Jews in Jesus' day. When He faced the Scribes and Pharisees it was quickly apparent that their views were diametrically opposed. When we brand a person as Pharisaical we usually mean that he is, in our estimation, a hypocrite. But Jesus faced a far bigger problem than a group of men whose prayers and practices did not

133

square. He was facing a great philosophy of life which exists to the present day.

To the Pharisees the Kingdom of God was a definite area and the business of religion was to run the division lines and place the corner posts and fence it in. Whoever strayed outside their fence was outside the Kingdom and whoever was inside their fence was inside the Kingdom. These religious leaders were confronted with a tremendous task, for they were compelled to survey all life down to the minutest act of the individual in every conceivable circumstance and say whether that act was inside or outside the fence. The common people were confused and perplexed because it required an expert theological surveyor to know where this ceremonial and traditional line ran amid the common tasks of life. The Pharisees and Scribes were busy keeping up the fences and explaining why they belonged in just this or that place.

It was into a situation such as this that Jesus came with his message of the New Order. He began his work with the announcement that the New Order was at hand. Almost at once He was questioned about the boundaries. Where did He propose to run them?

Mark's gospel gives, in interesting sequence, a series of attacks increasing in aggressiveness and bitterness during the early days of the Galilean ministry. The first clash came over the healing of a paralyzed man who was brought to Jesus by four friends (Mk. 2:1-12). Recognizing the faith of this man and his friends, Jesus said to the paralyzed man, "My son, your sins are pardoned." Immediately the Scribes who were present said, "Forgiveness doesn't come that way. This man must go to the priests and go through the prescribed ceremonies before there can be any forgiveness for him." These scribal experts knew just where the ceremonial fence ran which this man must climb before he could be forgiven, and they cried, "Blasphemy!" But Jesus seemed to say that God is not bound by man-made boundaries. He deals with men according to the inner facts of their lives. And to prove it He caused the life-giving, healing power of God to course through the man's paralyzed body.

The second clash was over a question of boundaries also (Mk. 2:13-17). Jesus had called Matthew the tax-gatherer to be his follower. In the eyes of all Jews this Matthew would be classed as a renegade. But Matthew was glad to follow Jesus, and he celebrated with a great feast, inviting the only friends he had, tax-gatherers and unchurched people like himself. Jesus was invited and accepted. That was a definite step outside the boundary lines, according to the religious leaders. "Doesn't your Master draw the line at men like these?" they asked Jesus' disciples. He said, "It is not the healthy who require a doctor, but the sick. I did not come to appeal to the righteous, but to sinners" (Mk. 2:17, Weymouth).

The third clash was about ceremonial. The religious leaders made use of the honest difficulty felt by the disciples of John because Jesus and his disciples did not fast (Mk. 2:18-22). They asked Him, "Do you mean to say that you don't even observe fast days?" They felt that all their fences were tumbling down. Jesus turned to John's disciples, we may well believe, and replied, "You will remember that your master John said I was the bridegroom and he was the bridegroom's friend (John 3:29). And you know

that friends of the bridegroom are released from the ceremonial regulations lest the joy of the occasion be marred."
These words He seemed to speak to meet the needs of
John's disciples; then He turns more to the Pharisees with
the words:

No one mends an old garment with a piece of unshrunk
cloth. Otherwise, the patch put on would tear away from
it—the new from the old—and a worse hole would be made.
And no one pours new wine into old wine-skins. Otherwise
the wine would burst the skins, and both wine and skins
would be lost. New wine needs fresh skins. (Mk. 2:21, 22,
Weymouth.)

This New Order was a new spirit too powerful and expan-
sive to be confined in old boundaries.

The fourth clash and the fifth follow in rapid succession
(Mk. 2:23-28; 3:1-6). They had to do with the field where
the Scribes had spent many a weary day running the division
fences, the field of Sabbath observance. And Jesus dis-
regarded the carefully erected divisions. You Pharisees, He
seemed to say, have missed the whole point of the matter.
You act as though man was made for the purpose of observ-
ing your traditions about the Sabbath. The opposite is the
case. The Sabbath was made to minister to the physical,
mental, and spiritual man (Mk. 2:27-28).

Time and again Jesus was asked where the boundary lines
ought to run. The Samaritan woman asked Him about places
for worshiping God, "Where does the line run? Does it
include Samaria or is Jerusalem the only proper place?"
And Jesus answered, "Believe me, the time is coming when
you will worship the Father neither on this mountain nor

in Jerusalem. . . . But a time is coming, nay, has already come, when the true worshipers will worship the Father with true spiritual worship" (John 4:21-23, Weymouth).

Peter brought up the old boundary question about forgiveness: "Master, how often shall my brother act wrongly toward me and I forgive him? Seven times?"

"I do not say seven times," answered Jesus, "but countless times" (Mt. 18:21, 22, Weymouth).

But Jesus' attitude toward this whole question of boundaries comes to clearest expression in the conversation with the wealthy ruler (Mk. 10:17-31). This man came running up to ask, "Good Master, what am I to do to inherit eternal life?" Jesus answered, "You know the boundaries, Do not murder, Do not commit adultery, Do not steal, and the rest." "Oh, yes," said the man, "I've kept inside the boundaries from my youth." "Then," said Jesus, "cut loose from everything and follow me."

When Jesus found a man who was tired of running boundary lines He invited him to leave the border country and visit the capital of the Kingdom of God. He issued no list of the boundary lines or the corner posts. No boundary line disputes vexed his soul, because He Himself lived at the capital of the Kingdom. The Scribes and Pharisees spent all their time thinking about disputes over divisions and limits and laws. Their eyes were fixed on the ground. They seem never to have discovered how very fair the Kingdom itself was. They were so busy warning folk about stepping over lines that they had not the time to describe the joys of the land, its running brooks and fertile fields and lofty hills, if indeed they themselves had ever noticed these attractions! But Jesus dwelt in the great interior regions of the Kingdom. He lived on the high plateaus and the broad plains where as far as the eye could reach it was all God's country. He dwelt at the capital of the Kingdom, the capital where God lives and men may see and know Him and hold friendly conversation with Him and receive strength and daily guidance for the business of living.

## II. The New Order Not a New Set of Laws.

We have thought of the New Order as the rule of God in the life of the individual, and we have discussed the ideal citizen and his inner attitude towards God and men and things. We have called this inner attitude the law of love. We have thought of the citizen as he faced society. But now we must go one step farther. What is to be the motive power behind this splendid program for the individual and for society? Is this program of the New Order another set of laws, another set of boundary lines, truer and straighter than the boundary lines of the Pharisees of old, but no less irksome and difficult, rather, vastly more difficult?

He who faces the program of the New Order as Jesus outlined it in the Sermon on the Mount will find it impossibly high and hard. All honor to the young man or woman who in the flush of idealism determines by the power of his own will to live out the Sermon on the Mount! But the odds are heavy against him. There was a young man who lived in the first century of the Christian era, the vigor of whose will and the energy of whose personality the world has not ceased to marvel at. But Paul confessed that a program of living vastly easier of accomplishment than the Christian program condemned him. He could not live up

138

to the letter of the Jewish law. Who will venture in his own strength to face the program of the New Order and live it out? As a program, as a law, as a set of boundary lines, it is impossibly hard.

Are we to suppose that Jesus of Nazareth did not know how high and hard the Sermon on the Mount is? Could He have lived in little Nazareth eighteen years, after that transforming experience at the temple, without discovering what human nature is like? Did He not battle with religious leaders who were crafty and selfish and hypocritical? Did He not understand that the multitude flocked to Him because He fed them or healed their diseases?

And what of his own disciples? How far short they fell of the ideal! It was two members of the inner circle, James and John, whose minds were filled with thoughts of worldly honor when they asked, "Allow us to sit one at your right hand and the other at your left, in your glory" (Mk. 10:37, Weymouth). And yet, in spite of it all, Jesus spoke these high and hard words, which have seemed the despair almost more than the hope of humanity. He offered no new set of laws as a substitute for the old. *He offered a new life.* Instead of a *program* He promised *power.* This New Order in its fair outlines was simply the characteristic way in which the new life would express itself. He dared to proclaim such a lofty way of life because He believed that there is a power available for common men and women beyond their own resources, which will enable them to live the life He outlined and make the New Order a reality on this earth.

### III. Sources of Power for the Citizen.

What are the sources of power without which this New Order is only a glittering dream?

Mark, with characteristic simplicity, reveals the principal source of power for that early group of disciples. In describing the selection of the Twelve Apostles he says, "He went up the hill; and those whom He Himself chose He called, and they came to Him. He appointed twelve of them that they might be with Him, and that He might send them to proclaim his message." Then follow the names of the twelve. In one-syllable words Mark reveals the primary reason why Jesus chose these men. It was in order *"that they might be with him."* He needed them and they needed Him vastly more, and so He called them into fellowship with Himself. Jesus avoided high-sounding titles during his ministry but He quietly took control of these men. He became their Lord and Master. All that they accomplished later they owed directly to Him, and they were the first to acknowledge it. They did not start out by being saints or theologians. They began by associating with Jesus.

No doubt they found the teaching of the Sermon on the Mount as high and hard as we find it to-day. They could no more live it out by might and main than can we. But as they fellowshipped with Him a marvelous thing happened. He lived Himself into their lives. His spirit permeated that group of men. They found themselves thinking about men and things and God as He thought about them.

And then came the terrible days when He set his face to go to Jerusalem to challenge for the last time the nation He loved better than his own life. They followed Him to

140

Jerusalem. They were dazed and bewildered by the tragic events that followed in quick succession, and with the crucifixion hope went out for them. They were like men who had followed a star over hill and dale until the star set and they were left to the darkness of despair. Intellectually they seem never to have understood Jesus and his message. They hoped to the last that He was to set up some sort of a material kingdom.

And yet nothing could separate them from the spirit of the Master. He had chosen these men "that they might be with Him," and even the terrible death of the Cross, with its black background of Jewish hate and Roman might could not tear Him from them. When the Easter morning broke with its message of amazing joy and hope, these men renewed their allegiance to the Lord and Master and faced a hostile world with triumphant faith. They began to live the Sermon on the Mount, not so much because they had accepted it as a program, as that the spirit of Jesus became the ruling motive in their lives. Paul put it most clearly when he said of his own experience, "It is as though I were no longer living but Christ were living in me."

What had happened to these men so to transform them? Jesus had led them to the capital of the New Order. They had been on a journey to the capital during the days and weeks in Judea and Galilee and Perea. The way grew rough and steep during the last terrible week in Jerusalem. And for a moment they seemed to have lost the path, but the light of the Easter morning illumined the way and at last they came to the city of God, the capital of the New Order, where God as a Father maintains his rule of love.

They learned by experience the meaning of Christ's words, "I am not alone, the Father is with me."

Such a profound inner experience came to these men in no mysterious fashion but in the simplest, most direct way. The spirit of Jesus became in a measure their own spirit, because they spent time with Him. They walked with Him, talked with Him, listened to his words and thought much about them. They held frequent friendly talks with Him, when the very secrets of their innermost lives were laid bare to his tender, healing, correcting gaze. They were lifted by this daily fellowship into something of the likeness of their Master.

In the same direct, simple fashion the spirit of Jesus becomes operative in the lives of men to-day. Nothing less than a constant fellowship with Him will lead us to the capital of the New Order. We are to listen to and ponder well his words, and how they cut through all pretense and shallowness and reveal the issues of life in our own time! We, too, must lay bare our inner lives to his purifying, strengthening gaze. We, too, must claim the privileges of daily comradeship with Him in prayer. And it may be, nay, it will be, that we shall be lifted into his likeness.

But he who has come to the capital of the New Order will find it to be a different sort of city than he had expected. The new spirit which fellowship with Christ creates is not in the least a spirit of self-satisfaction, even of spiritual satisfaction. It is the spirit, rather, of dissatisfaction with all the inequalities and injustices and wrongs of our common life. It is the spirit which leaps with joy at the unexampled opportunities for service to humankind which our world offers. It is a spirit which bids us stand shoulder to shoulder with Jesus as He reads to our stricken world the same message which came from his lips at Nazareth:

The Spirit of the Lord is upon me,
Because he has anointed me to proclaim Good News to the poor;
He has sent me to announce release to the prisoners of war
And recovery of sight to the blind;
To send away free those whom tyranny has crushed,
To proclaim the year of acceptance with the Lord.

But beyond Nazareth lay Calvary and the Cross. When He spoke those wonderful words at Nazareth He accepted the possibility of a Cross at the end of the road. As the Cross is the symbol of entire devotion to the will of God it was the symbol of his whole life. He did not accept the Cross because He could not escape it. He stedfastly set his face toward it. He poured out his life in the accomplishment of the glorious program which He had read in the Nazareth synagogue, confident that God's way to victory is the way of utter devotion, whatever the cost. The resurrection was and is God's affirmation of the sublime truth.

Following Jesus Christ will mean, then, not only standing shoulder to shoulder with Him as He pronounces to our world the message of individual release and social blessing, but also following Him even to the Cross of utter self-sacrifice, confident that God will grant us through Jesus Christ that same assurance of victory.

# A TEACHING OUTLINE

# "THE WAY OF CHRIST"

## GENERAL SUGGESTIONS

1. Get a general view of the course by reading the entire book through, noting the points that especially apply to the problems of your group.
2. Study the Biblical material first and then the material of the chapter. If you find that you differ with the author, go back to the Bible and see where he gives you additional help.
3. In planning the discussional hour :—
   a. Try to make your own outline before you refer to the one suggested.
   b. Begin with the part of the topic that will interest the group most and lead on from that.
   c. Make the discussion as general as possible by asking questions to make people think (see Strayer : Short Course in the Teaching Process, Chapter on "Questioning") or by getting many opinions on a point.
4. Ask yourself after each discussional hour : "What questions have we found help in answering? What new questions have been raised?"

## TEACHING OUTLINE FOR USE OF THE LEADER

### Introductory Lesson.

(For which no preparation has been made and in which time must be taken for organization of the group; yet the discussion must be interesting enough to claim attention from the first.)

### Preparation.

1. Look up the Biblical references given in the suggestions for Personal Study for Chapter I and read the chapter carefully.

2. Supplement this description of the kind of people among whom Jesus spent his childhood and boyhood, by reading as many of the following references as possible:

Glover: Jesus of History, Chapter II.

Smith: Days of His Flesh, pp. 2-24.

Kent: Historical Bible, Volume V (Life and Teachings of Jesus, pp. 43-56).

Any good life of Christ which will give you a picture of the contrast between the worldly Pharisees and the simple, devout peasants among whom Jesus lived.

3. What were the principal elements in the environment of Jesus' childhood and boyhood?

### Discussional Hour.

1. How much do the circumstances in which a person spends his childhood and the people he knows influence him? Should a person say, "I can't help it, I was brought up that

way"? What is the place of will in growth? What environ-ment would you choose for a child who was to be a leader? What would you consider most important?

2. What were some of the characteristics of Jesus' envi-ronment? (Get what ideas the group have and then refer to this question the next hour.)

3. What influence would people like Zachariah, Elizabeth and Mary be likely to have? (Have the members of the group read Luke 1:5-6; 46-55, 67-79.) How well was Jesus acquainted with the great religious leaders of his nation in the past? (Isa. 29:13 with Mk. 7:9; Hosea 6:6 with Mt. 9:13.) What influence would you expect this to have?

### Assignment Questions.

Why should Luke have chosen only one incident in the boyhood of Jesus to tell us? (He was not careless in his choice of material. Bring out this point by referring to Luke 1:1-4.) Does graduation mark the beginning of a life work? When did Jesus' life work begin? (Study for next time Luke 2:40-52.) What was the importance of his home training, the religious thinking of his day, his own awakening understanding? (Study Chapter I.)


## CHAPTER I

**Theme:** What effect has the "set" of a life on the future?

### Preparation.

1. Re-study the. material of the chapter and jot down the main points you wish to bring out in the discussion.

2. Picture to yourself the incident recorded in Luke 2:40-52, thinking carefully of its relation to his later call. What experiences may a girl or boy have to-day that would be comparable to Jesus' experience in the Temple?

3. Read Luke 1:5-25; 57-80. Contrast the preparation of John with that of Jesus. Plan to bring out the points in the preparation of Jesus which next week will make this contrast clear to the girls (i.e., Jesus grew up among the people of a small town in every day human relationships. Next week you will need this point to contrast with John's desert background).

## THE DISCUSSIONAL HOUR

1. a. Begin with the assignment questions given out last week. Find out what the group thinks about the time when a life work begins.

b. If you think every one has not read the chapter, review it briefly, trying to picture clearly the visit to the Temple and the discussion with the teachers; what they talked about, etc. Get this from the group, if possible, but do not spend more than a third of the discussional hour on it.

2. What hopes and ideals have we to-day that are as challenging to us as those of Jesus' day were to Him? (See Chapter I, Sec. 2: Fosdick's "Challenge of the Present Crisis"; Dawson's "Carry On.") How much of the whole meaning of "Christian world democracy" need we understand before determining to make it our life job? Why does be ginning to work at a thing make it easier to understand?

3. What did the "silent years" do for Jesus? What char-

acterizes the "silent years" of the average student,—restless impatience, indifferent "drifting," or steady, purposeful growth? Why are students being urged to finish college instead of going at once into war work? If Jesus could afford to wait quietly for his call in the face of the Jewish crisis, cannot we?

4. What is the difference between pledging a part of our time and work, and pledging ourselves? Which gives "set" to a life? We are being asked in these days to give time and money constantly. Is there a greater gift we have still? Are we keeping for ourselves the greatest gift,—"an unex hausted, untainted potential personality"? Has our "Father's business" become of supreme importance to us?

5. What testing did Jesus' purpose meet? How much would mine stand?

## Assignment Questions.

6. a. In what ways does the call to action come to those who have already "set" their lives? What is the significance of John as the "forerunner of Jesus"? Who are some of the forerunners of our day? (Socialists, labor agitators, etc.?) What made John great enough to be always remembered? (Read Mt. 3: 1-12; Mk. 1: 1-8.)

b. How did his preparation differ from that of Jesus? Does a different job demand different preparation? (Read Luke 1: 5-25, 57-80.)

c. What constitutes a call to leadership? (Mk. 1: 0-11.)

d. How shall we test the greatness of leadership? (Mt. 4: 1-11.)

## CHAPTER II

**Preparation.**

1. Get clearly before your own mind the contrast between the "silent years" of Jesus and of John. Try to see John through the eyes of a peasant Jew of that time—like Andrew, for instance. (Biblical references and material of Chapter II.)

2. Think out the points to be made on the following topics and word your own questions before comparing them with those suggested under "Discussional Hour":

   a. The elements that make up an ideal preparation for citizenship in the New Order.

   b. The difference between being the Great Herald of the New Order and a citizen in it.

   c. The adequacy of John's message for the world situation of to-day. The further need of Christ-like leadership.

   d. The reality of the temptation to self-gratification, popularity and compromise, and the concrete ways they manifest themselves. The characteristics of Christ-like leadership.

**Discussional Hour.**

1. What kind of environment would you choose as a preparation for citizenship in the New Order? (Refer to Chapter I.) Compare the preparation of Lincoln with that of President Wilson. Compare the preparation of John with that of Jesus. What are the necessary elements that any kind of preparation must have?

2. Can a man be the herald of a great cause and yet not have a part in its final accomplishment? Can you illustrate from college life? What is the difference between being the Herald of the New Order and a citizen in it? Compare the relation of Jesus and John to the New Order.

3. Read in class Luke 3 : 1-20. Has the convincing note of hope, and the challenge to conscience any parallel in our day? What? Can what we are fighting for be attained with out both of these? Do they together constitute an adequate message for our times? Why? What more is needed besides a message? Why did John also proclaim his own secondary place of leadership? What was there in the preaching of John to call Jesus from Nazareth? What is the significance of Christ-like leadership to-day?

4. Get the group to re-state the temptations of Jesus in modern terms. To what extent does every leader face these same temptations? By what three tests shall we judge the greatness of leadership? What do you believe to be the essential characteristics of leadership in the New Order?

## Assignment Questions.

5. How does one go to work to establish any New Order of things (such as student government, honor system, etc.)? How far can a popular movement be utilized? What shall we do with the Old Order? Which is harder—to destroy it or build on it? Which is better? How are we to meet failure, opposition and popularity? To follow up this question look up the Suggestions for Personal Study, Chapter III.

## CHAPTER III

**Theme:** Our methods of establishing the New Order must be statesmanlike as Jesus' were.

### Preparation.

1. The "Suggestions for Study" might be used by the leader as a guide in planning the discussional hour after the chapter has been carefully studied.

Emphasize concrete illustrations from your own campus.

2. Or, the discussional hour may be planned as suggested below.

### Discussional Hour.

1. Under what circumstances can a "new order" (such as student government or the honor system) be successfully started? Can you think of any college reforms that have failed because the leaders were too impatient? Compare this with Jesus' patient waiting until the crusade of John gave Him an opening. How can the widespread desire to give patriotic service help us to a deeper understanding of Christian service as a purpose for the whole of our lives?

2. How far can an "old order" be utilized in building the new one? Compare Mt. 3:1-12 with Mk. 1:14-15 and Luke 15:11-24. What elements in John's message did Jesus use in his earlier preaching? Did He later stress other things more? What elements in such popular movements as socialism, the labor movement, etc., can be used in establishing a Christian democracy in the world?

3. The establishment of a new order is never clear sailing. What effect do apparent failure, opposition or popularity usually have on people? How do *you* believe they can be met? Illustrate from your own campus or community.

How did Jesus meet opposition, apparent failure or popularity? (See Secs. 2 and 3 of the chapter.) If the group is not fairly familiar with the chapter, you could distribute the following references and questions on slips of paper and give them five minutes to think them over ·

   a. John 2: 13-22. Try to imagine what it would mean to Jesus to come back to the Temple where He had listened to the scholars to find it the center of legalized graft.
   b. John 4: 1-2. How would Jesus feel about the rivalry that threatened the "friendship which had made possible the beginnings of his work"?
   c. Why was it "statesmanlike acumen" on Jesus' part to turn to Galilee after the failure in Judea?
   d. Skim through the first chapter of Mark and pick out what evidence you find of the rapid popularity of Jesus in Galilee.
   e. Illustrate the opposition of the Pharisees from any incidents you remember.
   f. How did Jesus change the character of his teaching in order to sift the crowd? Mark 4: 12.
   g. Having faced apparent failure, opposition and popularity, what course was left to Him?

4. Why was Jesus "never so truly the statesman as when He set his face to go to Jerusalem"? What is the "statesmanship of sacrifice"?

### Assignment Questions.

What do you believe the world most needs to-day? In your own college? In your own community?

## CHAPTER IV

**Theme:** Why does Jesus' idea of the New Order offer us hopes for the future?

### Preparation.

1. Think back over all the articles relating to the present crisis that you have read and get clearly before your mind what seem to you the three or four greatest needs the world has to-day. If possible refer to "The Challenge of the Present Crisis" by Fosdick.

2. Now try to study the Biblical references as if you had never seen them before and were looking at them as a brand-new suggestion for the solution of our present problems. Characterize the main points for yourself.

3. After these two steps you will be ready to study the chapter and to add to your notes what you think will especially need to be brought out with your group. Use some of the questions in the "Suggestions for Personal Study" in making your outline for the discussional hour.

### Discussional Hour.

1. Get from the group their ideas of the supreme need of the world to-day. In what words do we express our aims

and hopes for the future? What do *we* call the New Order? Jesus used the terminology familiar to his nation. What was his name for it?

2. Give each member of the group a chance to report on the references which they have studied. Then have the outstanding characteristics of the New Order as Jesus set it forth summed up. Use a blackboard if possible.

3. Choose one topic, such as The New Order's Inestimable Value (or more if you have time), and see what significance it would have to-day. What values to-day are men willing to die for?

4. Go back to your discussion of the supreme need of the world as you saw it and compare with Jesus' teaching about the New Order. Why should Christians believe that the New Order will fulfill the world's need?

### Assignment Questions.

What part will this group have in establishing such a New Order? What are the conditions of citizenship that must first be met?

Study these individual cases and think out the conditions:

(a) Mk. 1 : 16-20; 2 : 13, 14.

(b) Mk. 5 : 18-20 (esp. v. 19).

(c) Luke 19 : 1-10.

(d) Mt. 19 : 16-20.

## CHAPTER V

**Theme:** What will bring about the "transformed and energized personality" necessary to living in the New Order?

**Preparation.**

1. Look up everything you can find about the experiences of such men as Grenfell and Moody in becoming citizens of the New Order. Other references to use are ·

Burton: Comrades in Service; Notable Women of Modern China.

Begbie: Twice Born Men

2. Study the stories of some of the men who became citizens in Jesus' own day and Jesus' own teaching about citizenship. What do *you* think are the conditions? (See "Suggestions for Personal Study")

3. When you study the chapter see if you and the author differ about the conditions of citizenship. Find out why he thinks as he does.

**Discussional Hour.**

1. What do we expect of a new student in his attitude towards the college? Of a new member in a fraternity? Why are we especially indignant at "hyphenated Americans"? What does citizenship in a college or the United States mean?

2. Jesus called men to citizenship in a New Order. Let members of the group tell the stories of the Gerasene de-

moniac, the fishermen and Matthew, Zaccheus, and the rich young man. Can you pick out from these stories the conditions of citizenship? When the group has brought out as many points as possible, distribute the different references given in the first part of the Biblical Material (to give further light on such points as: Repent and believe, appreciation, receptivity, counting the cost, etc.). How would you describe the conditions of citizenship in terms of to-day to one who was not a Christian?

3. Take such key phrases as the following:
Repentance,—"that moral renovation of the entire life."
Belief,—"the launching of the entire personality in the service of the Kingdom."

4. Can you find any cases where fulfilling the conditions did not result in a transformed life? Did Jesus expect it to always express itself in the same way? (Recall the Gerasene demoniac versus the fishermen). How would the "transformed life" manifest itself in your college or community if men should actually follow the leadership of Jesus?

Who are the people to-day who answer the call of Jesus for such a transformation in life purposes and attitudes? Are they all among those we call Christians? What is holding men back from full citizenship in the New Order? Can we expect that the New Order will make less exacting demands than our own country at war?

### Assignment Questions.

What kind of a person would *you* call an "ideal citizen"?
Can you re-write Mt. 5: 1-12 in modern terms? Bring it to the next discussion hour.

## CHAPTER VI

**Theme:** Will the Ideal Citizen as Jesus pictured him satisfy us in the New Order for which we hope?

**Preparation.**

1. If you have a half-acknowledged idea that the Ideal Citizen pictured in Mt. 5: 1-12 is a rather impossible person whom nobody would want to be or know (and many of us if we are honest have to confess to some such idea), you may be pretty sure that your group thinks the same way and you will want to answer the question in the Theme for yourself in order to help them think it out.

2. Why not begin by thinking of the people in your college or community whom you believe make the best citizens? (Keep in mind Jesus' idea of a new order and your conclusions after studying Chap. IV.) What characteristics stand out especially? What do you mean by power? How is it different from bluster? Why do we use the words "quiet power"? Who are the most powerful people you know?

Then think back over a month of college and see where an ideal citizen would have acted differently from any of the students you know.

3. Describe to yourself an ideal citizen in the new order we are trying to establish. Re-write the Beatitudes in terms of to-day. How near alike are the two pictures?

4. This week make your own outline for the discussion

hour, working in any of the following questions that you need.

### Discussional Hour.

Questions that may be used by leader in planning the hour:

What is an ideal Freshman (or Sophomore, Junior or Senior) like?

How many characteristics that belong to the ideal citizen of a college (or any other community) can you find in Jesus' picture of the ideal citizen? (Mt. 5: 1-12.)

When you look at Jesus (who was genuinely the Ideal Citizen) what does meekness (humility) mean? Did He lack force of character? (Read in class John 2: 13-16.)

What new meanings can you find for the other Beatitudes when you study Jesus?

What would happen if people and nations used this ideal of citizenship as a working principle?

### Assignment Questions.

Which is easier as a citizen of a college to-day, to obey a set of rules made for you or to abide by the attitude of self-government? Which gets the best results? Why?

Can you tell from the 5th and 6th chapters of Matthew what Jesus gave his friends instead of rules?

## CHAPTER VII

**Theme:** Not rules but attitudes mark the Ideal Citizen as Jesus described him.

# THE WAY OF CHRIST

**Preparation.**

1. When you have answered the first three questions in the suggested assignment, you will be ready to read the introduction to the chapter. What does the author add to your conclusions?

2. In three parallel columns on a note-book page headed "The Ideal Citizen's Attitude Towards (1) People, (2) Things, (3) God" jot down, as you find it in studying the references given in the Biblical material, whatever makes the inner attitude of the Ideal Citizen different from that of one not a citizen. If you use abstract words like "graciousness" be sure to illustrate with concrete incidents and use the chapter material after the Bible itself.

### Discussional Hour.

1. Get the opinion of the group on the relative values of a set of rules and self-government. Will copying the manners and clothes of a popular student make an unpopular student liked? What will? Tell the group the story of "The Frogs."

2. Divide the group into three parts, give one the references for the citizen's attitude towards "people," one those for "things" and the third those for "God." Suggest that they take ten minutes to determine the inner attitudes towards "people" (fellow students, professors, maids in dormitories, foreigners, under-classmen, etc.), towards "things" (examinations, "eats," clothes, societies, etc.) and towards God, that mark the Ideal Citizen.

You may want also to use such questions as:

Why is it so hard to get along with people?

How does my attitude towards the foreign student resemble that of the small boy who calls "Chink" after him? How far is such an attitude in the world responsible for the war?

How would "simplicity" as an attitude towards "things" affect both cramming for or bluffing through an examination?

. Does *my* life "consist in" the number of societies to which I belong? Does a nation's life "consist in" the proportion of its commercial power?

3. Ask each part of the group to report their discussion in three minutes apiece.

How would you summarize the inner attitude of the Ideal Citizen? (See Mt. 6:33.)

Can the war be truly "won" until this "search" becomes the "consuming passion" of *our* lives? Where and when does the "search" begin?

**Assignment Questions.**

What fundamental law guides this search which is to carry us into new relationships with people and God? Can you translate I Cor. 13 into modern college terms?

"It has always been orthodox to believe in loving one's neighbor, but it has always been startling when people really tried to do it." Will you try this week to find out by experiment just how "startling" it is to apply honestly the fundamental law of love?

## CHAPTER VIII

**Theme:** The law of love is the motive power of the New Order applicable to each part of its program.

**Preparation.**

1. Paul did not give a definition of love in I Cor. 13, but he did tell what resulted when you made it the motive. Read I Cor. 13 through slowly in either the Weymouth or Moffatt translations.

2. Our author suggests certain popular notions of what love is. What happens when we think of it as "amicable dooryard diplomacy," "emergency legislation," etc.? (See chapter material.) Study the references in Biblical material (2) and (3). Have you thought before of brotherhood and love? Are they the same?

3. Review the summary the group made of Chapters V and VI. What meaning for "love" will make it an effective motive power for such citizenship?

**Discussional Hour.**

1. From your experiments this week can you suggest why the world has never been willing to accept the fundamental law of Christianity?

2. Is love a sentiment? Is it "emergency legislation"? "amicable dooryard diplomacy"? Get the group to illustrate these incomplete definitions of love and tell why they do not work. What meaning for love does brotherhood express?

3. What kind of person would this law produce if it be-

came the motive power of a life? Compare with your study of the Ideal Citizen and his inner attitudes. How far will this work between nations? Illustrate from the programs of the "League for Peace," a "league of nations." etc.

### Assignment Questions.

Can the law of love be made effective by individual citizens working separately? Why? Before next week try to paraphrase Luke 4: 16-22 as expressing Jesus' idea of the way citizens of the New Order will go to work. Who are our "blind"? Are all our "prisoners" in Germany? How are we to "free" those in Sing Sing prison?

## CHAPTER IX

**Theme:** The result in a society of citizens working to-
    gether for the New Order.

### Preparation.

Supplement the "Suggestions for Personal Study" with any of the following references·

Ward: Social Creed of the Churches, Chap. IV.

Scudder: Church and the Hour, Introduction.

Rauschenbusch: Christianizing the Social Order.

Reports of the Child Labor Bureau (sent from Washing-
    ton on request).

Current numbers of *The Survey.*

### Discussional Hour.

1. Which is more to blame, the student who cheats in examination or the public opinion of the college which

encourages him "not to let his work interfere with his college education"? Where does the burden of responsibility rest for the girl who seeks unsafe amusement, with the girl or the community which fails to provide a chance for clean fun? Can you suggest other questions like these? (Use illustrations given in the chapter.)

2. Have two or three in the group read their paraphrases of Luke 4: 16-22. Draw out (by questions chosen from the Suggestions for Personal Study or worded by the leader beforehand) a discussion of what responsibility Christians have for the "poor," those who are "prisoners," etc.

3. Why should we be working together as Ideal Citizens? What is our goal? What tools have we to use? (Legislation, playgrounds, etc.) Will these things alone accomplish our purpose? What bearing has this on our discussion of inner attitudes? Will the right inner attitude come by waiting while we leave undone the task of "bearing one another's burdens"?

## Assignment Questions.

Is Christianity a matter of "oughts" and "ought nots"? We say frequently, "I draw the line." Where? At what people and actions? When do boundary lines become unnecessary?

## CHAPTER X

**Theme:** The New Order of Jesus can become the new order for our world just because it is not a *new program* but a *new life.*

## A TEACHING OUTLINE

**Preparation.**

In addition to the Suggestions for Personal Study read Glover: Jesus of History, Chap. V (Also Chap. III and IV if possible.)

### Discussional Hour.

1. Use the questions at the end of the previous hour to start the discussion, drawing out a few of our special "boundary lines" (our "oughts" and "ought nots"), but try not to take more than six or seven minutes on this point. What Pharisaical traditions exist in the average college? How do these correspond with the "boundary lines" of Jesus' day?

2. Unless the group has studied the chapter thoroughly enough to discuss it, first give out the following references on slips of paper to be read over in five minutes:

Mk. 2: 1-12; Mk. 2: 13-17; Mk. 2: 18-22; Mk. 2: 23-28; Mk. 3: 1-6; Mt. 18: 21-22; Mk. 10: 17-31.

What was Jesus' answer to the rich young ruler as our author paraphrases it? Why does not such "cutting loose" end in disaster? What is the difference between this and ·license?

3. The world has tried programs and failed. Why will a "new life" succeed? Would it be easier to live in the spirit of the Beatitudes or according to the Jewish law? Why? What made the friends of Jesus eager to attempt the harder task and increasingly triumphant in it?

4. Are we honestly willing to test our desire for the coming of the New Order by the measure of our commitment to fellowship with Jesus, not alone when the crowds hung

on his words, but also when He "set his face to go to Jerusalem"?

## REVIEW LESSON

The last discussional hour should be truly a *"re-*view" of the questions raised and answered in the previous discussions. Only two or three ways of doing this are suggested here. What others can you think of?

1. Ask the members of the group to bring with them the three most significant questions raised in the course.

2. Work out with the group the main points you would try to make in explaining Jesus' New Order to a Japanese factory worker or to a Chinese student.

3. Try to write a prayer that a citizen of the New Order might pray. (Remember the perfect prayer, but do not merely copy.)